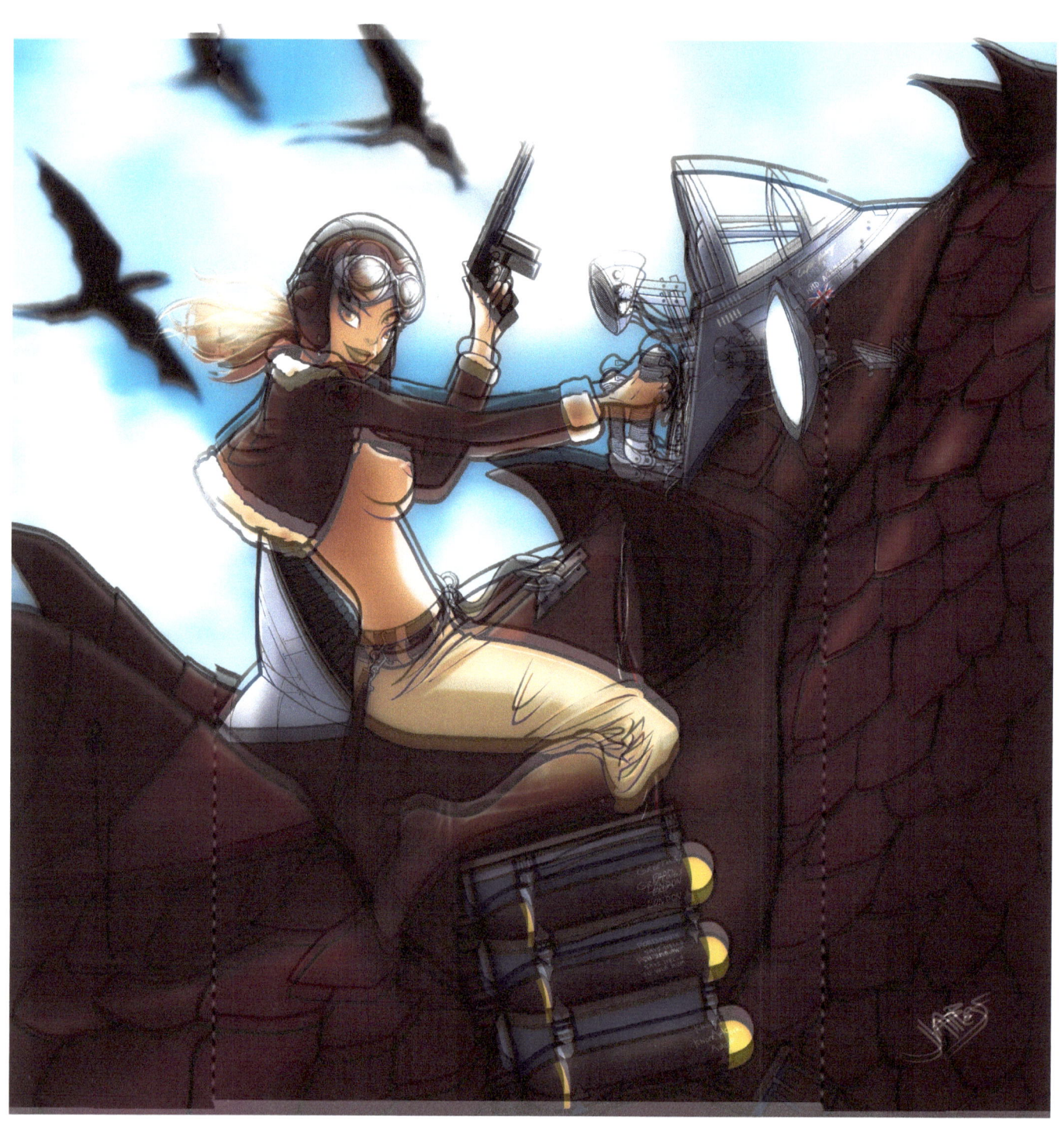

Capt. Naomi Aubrey, of the Royal Aerial Corps, astride Agamemnon, third of his name.

# Firebombshell

Agamemnon, as a rare heavyweight Regulus Wyvern, assumed the role of Wing Commander upon his formal entry into the service, due to the central role of heavy bombers in the British attack wing. Lacking the combat experience of some of his fellow fighters (his wing mate, Athena, had served in the first Boer War), it was important that his Captain possess the wisdom, discipline and tactical mastery that he did not.

Fortunately, Captain Aubrey had those in spades. Relatively seasoned for an aviator during WW2, she had been a teenage Ensign during the Third Afghan War in 1919 aboard the famed Regulus, Heracles. Furthermore, as a direct descendant of Rear Admiral "Lucky Jack" Aubrey, she came from a long line of military commanders.

No accident, then, that she became Agamemnon's captain, as dragon commands are largely hereditary. Several heavyweight dragon species will only accept female riders, and are most keen to adopt the daughters of present captains as their future captains, or reserve them for their progeny. Because the rules of promotion are so complex and dependent on the availability and preferences of the dragons themselves, the Royal Aerial Corps were long-considered the "red-headed stepchild" of the King's Armed Forces, shunned by career soldiers looking for a less capricious path to advancement. Ever since St. George and the Princess of Silene befriended the dragon, inaugurating centuries of human-dragon cooperation in War, dragon-riding soldiers had been an insular group largely ignored by the "more respectable" services. Uncertain career prospects were far from the only reason for the Aerial Corps' neglect before WW2: fear of the creatures, and fear of the sexually liberated females that the Corps bred also played a large role.

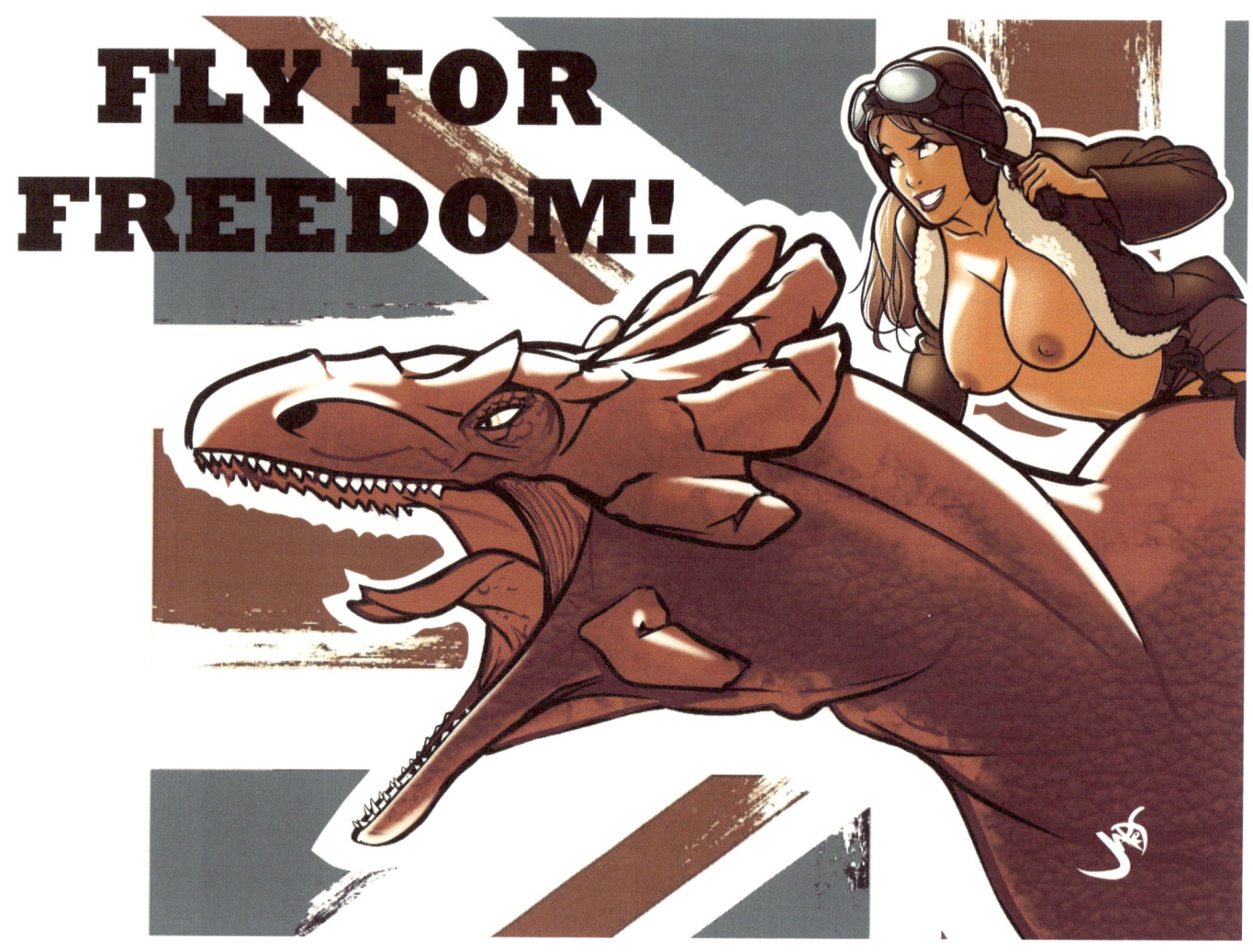

Though they were instrumental in the British victory in the Napoleonic Wars (owing to certain species of Dreadnaught-class dragons only bonding with female riders), female aviators were slow to be accepted in larger society, the scandalized public believing the back of a dragon to be far too rough a place for a proper British lady. It was only with the existential threat of Axis dragons crossing the Channel to firebomb London and Portsmouth that the general public began to accept the necessity of women contributing to the war effort in the Aerial Corps.

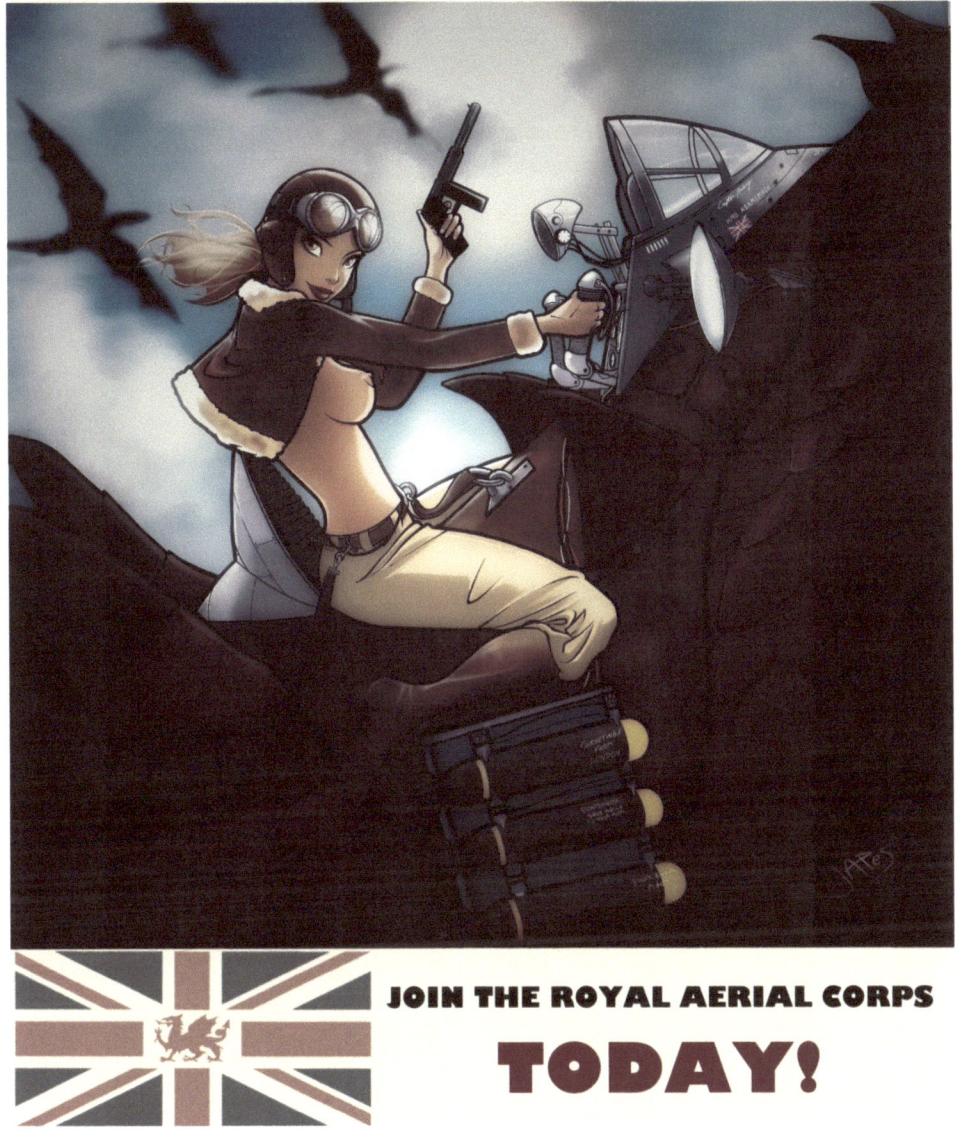

Recruitment posters such as this (meant to lure those British women who felt constrained by corsets and propriety with promises of freedom and liberation) also proved to quintuple the enlistment of young men from as far away as America. The scores of young men and women who joined the Corps, eager to see what promised to be the most sexually liberated service, helped turned the tide of The Battle of Britain, and ultimately the course of the War.

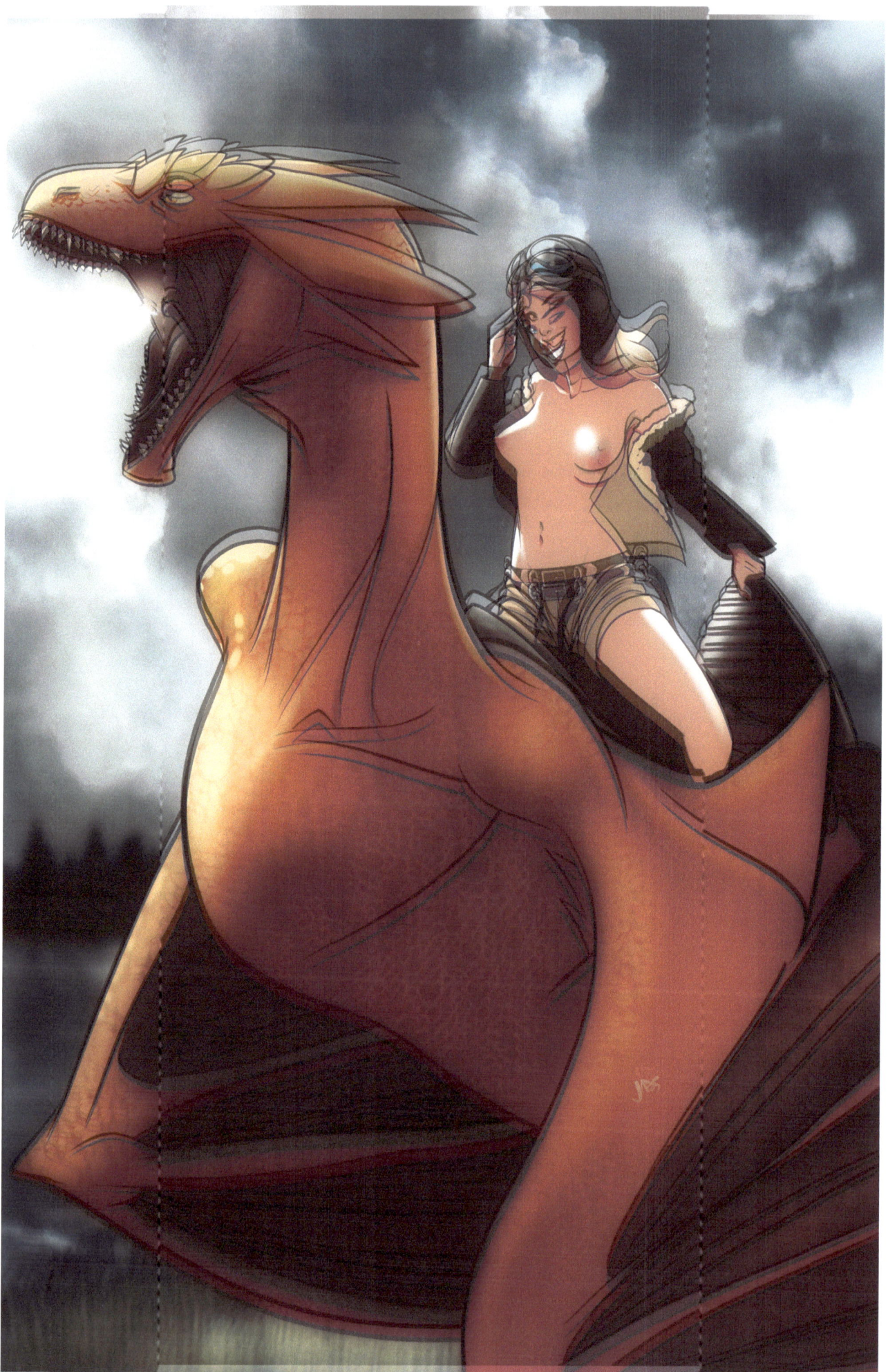

# SALUTE!

The Corps was adept at assigning different combat roles to different dragon species, according to their strengths. From the hulking Regulus Wyverns like Agamemnon, (literally the most powerful creature in the world) who could carry a crew of seven, plus several tonnes of bombs, to the fast, nimble single-rider Lightning Shrike, like Helios, every combat role was filled with a dragon species well-suited to its task.

Lightning Shrikes were deployed ahead of a bomber sortie, and tasked with wiping out enemy Anti-Dragon (AD) defenses. As a species, Lightning Shrikes were capable of both instant changes in direction, and prolonged hovering. In the wild, they shared a hunting technique with their namesake birds — shepherds would report a sheep grazing peacefully in a meadow, then a crimson blur and a second later, the sheep would be impaled at the top of a tree, to be consumed at leisure later while it hunted for more. Absolutely vicious in combat, Lightning Shrikes were virtually impossible for anti-flyer defenses to hit; they simply waltzed through flak as if it were stationary, grabbed the AD gun by its barrel, tore it off and swatted the AD crew with it, then moved on. The only effective defense for an AD battery was effective camouflage, as Shrike vision was motion-sensitive and they had trouble picking out stationary, disguised targets.

Like her dragon, Captain Agathon was a stone-cold killer underneath a beautiful, bright exterior. She was known to smile grimly while Helios tore German crews apart, mentally subtracting one less threat to her friends in Agamemnon's wing above.

Opposite: Captain Cassandra "Cassie" Agathon aboard Helios

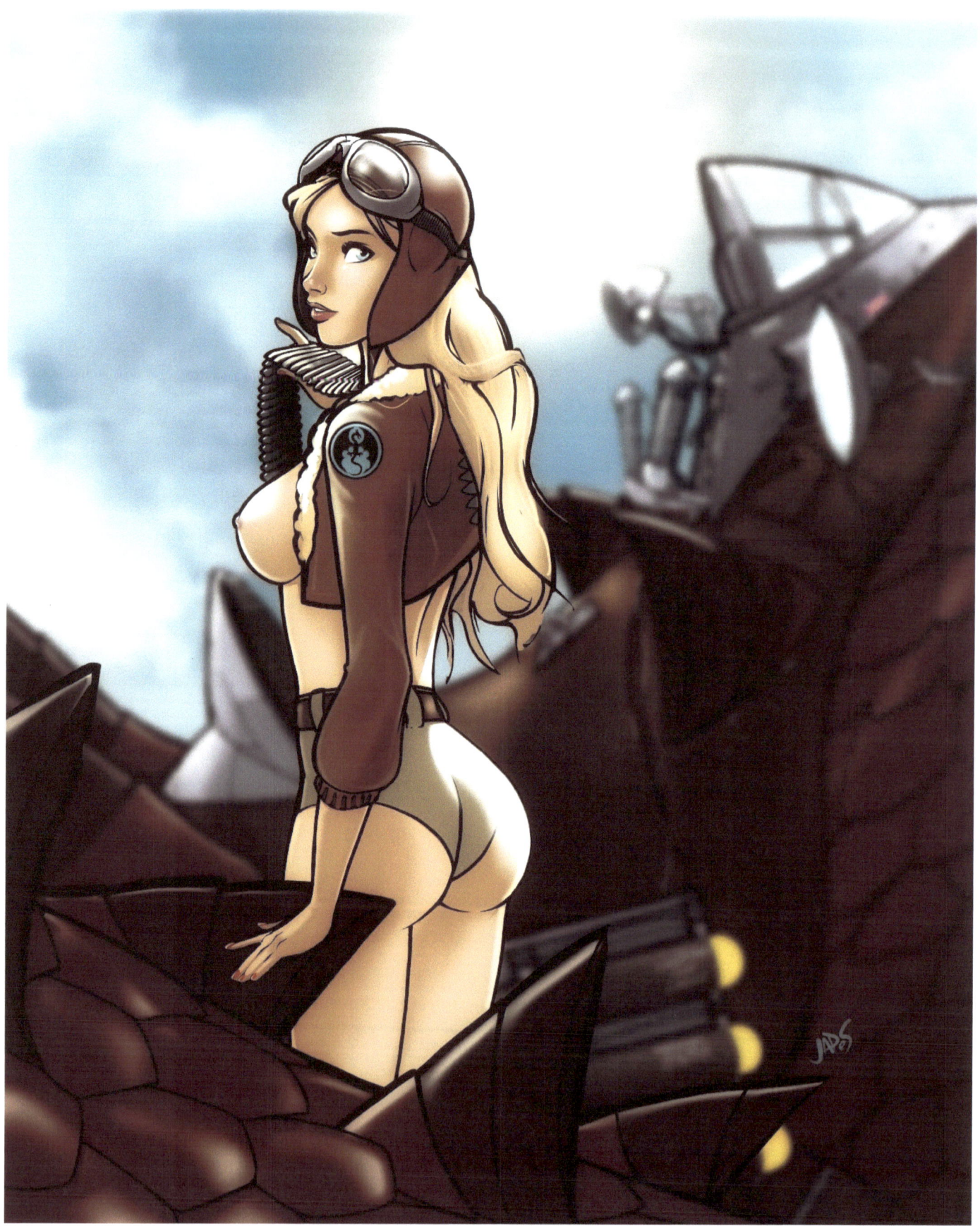

# TAIL GUNNER

Defying the usual Hobbesian lifespan of tail gunners during the Second Great War, (whose firing position at the base of a dragon's tail proved to be the most vulnerable to enemy fire and smaller dragon attacks) Elliott "Ellie" St. James survived the war in part due to the fierce attachment her dragon developed for her.

Agamemnon guarded her as jealously as he would any jewel, as he prized her not only for her excellent marksmanship in keeping enemy fliers off his tail, but also as a particularly attractive breeding female to help swell the ranks of his crew. A main determinant of dragon status in the Royal Aerial Corps was the size of their crew; they hoarded human ground and flight crew much like the dragons of old hoarded precious gems, and the most illustrious dragons could boast of several generations of captains springing from the interbreeding of their crew. Agamemnon constantly

worried about the brash young Lieutenant covering his six, and had a habit of lifting his tail to cover her when he felt the attacks coming from the rear becoming too hot. He then patiently endured the stings of bullets from the enemy and later the fusillade of swearing from young Ellie as she upbraided him for yet again spoiling her shot.

Captain Aubrey had to suppress a smile when witnessing the scene of the headstrong young woman dressing down the 22-ton dragon. Normally she would have corrected the dragon too, but she could hardly blame him, having developed a soft spot of her own for the young Lieutenant...

Opposite: Ellie St. James with Agamemnon

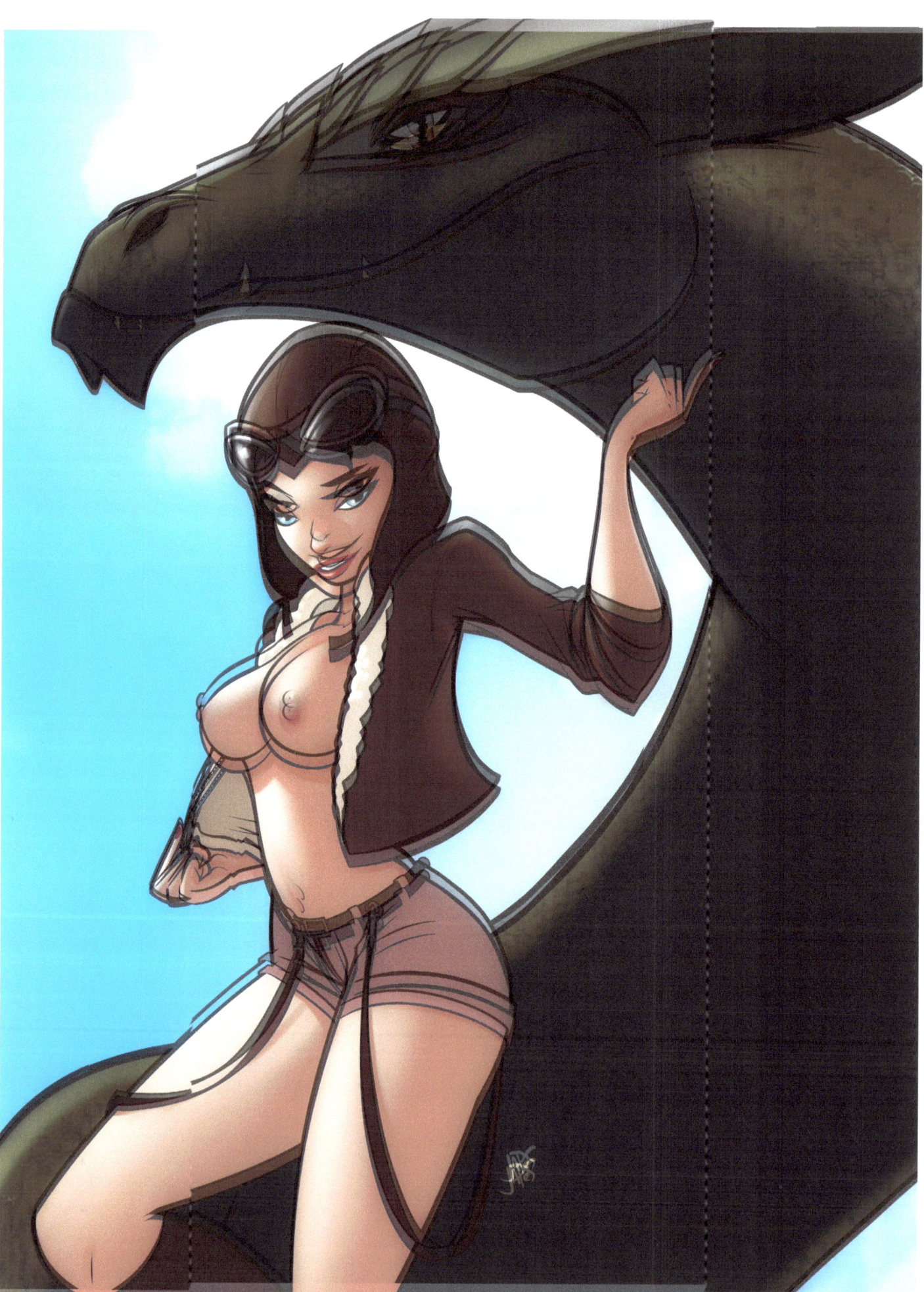

# Come Hither

When I first started out painting the women of the Corps, I had just come from painting dames on the sides of tanks, and was still very much in that mode. When I showed the subjects of this piece, Captain Lana King, and her dragon Hector, the finished work, she was bemused and a little grateful that no one would recognize her from this cartoonish likeness. Hector, however, was very upset at his likeness, complaining that he didn't look like that at all, and that I had failed to capture his power and majesty in "that silly doodle." I learned then that dragons don't really "get" the concept of caricature, and as having a several tonne dragon miffed at you is not an experience soon forgotten, my style changed in a hurry after that.

Opposite: Captain King with Hector

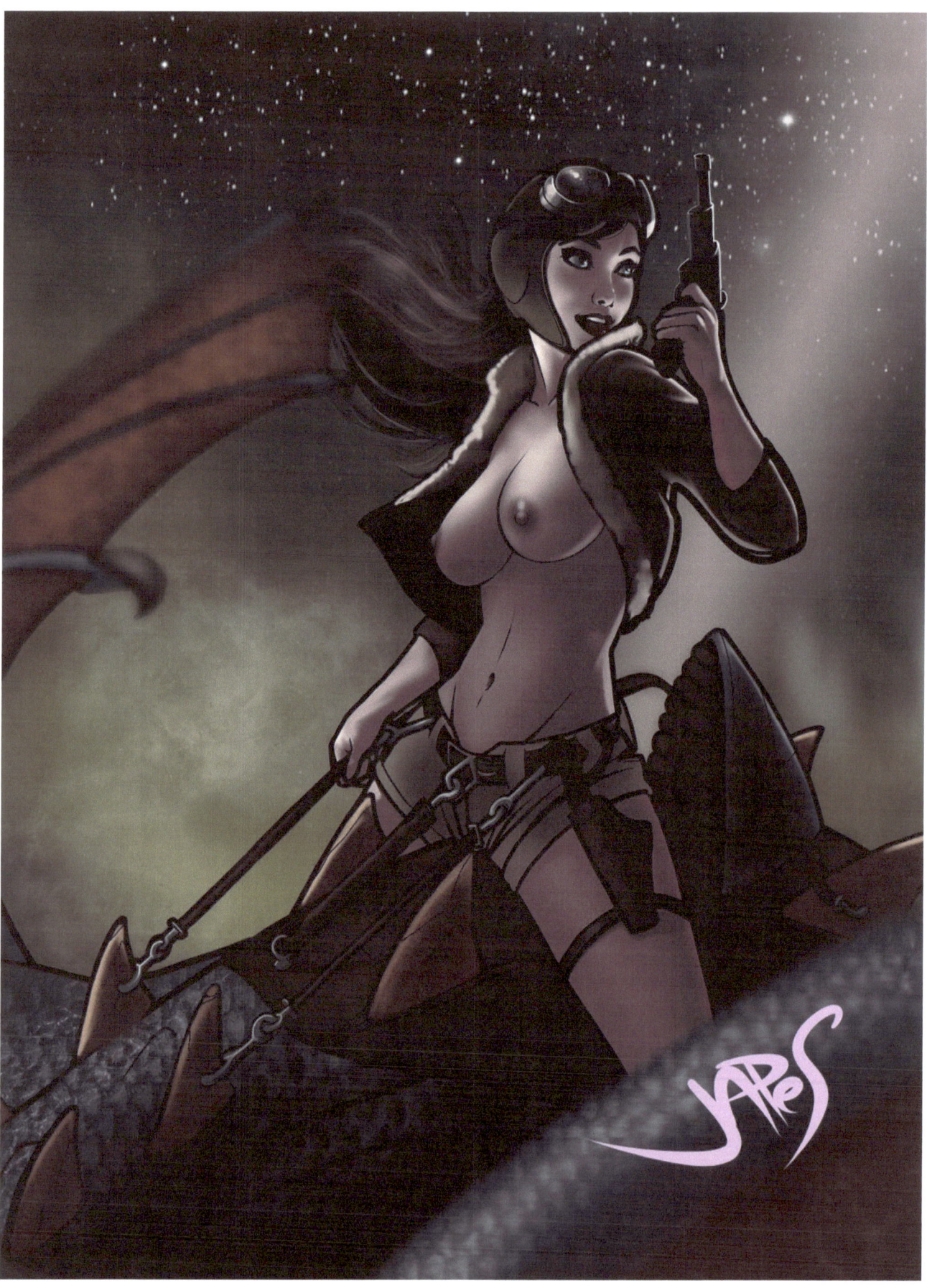

# Night Patrol

Named for their distinctive crest, which acts as a receiver for the echoes bouncing off their prey and their environment, Crested Shriekers are erratic flyers, uninterested in maintaining formation and unable to maintain any target discipline. Thus, they proved unsuitable for use in any attack sorties, but invaluable as flying radar, given their unique echolocation abilities and ability to stay aloft all night long patrolling the territory around their nests. They proved such adept sentries that the nighttime Axis firebombing raids over British cities soon became largely ineffective wastes of dragons and ordinance, the element of surprise effectively lost once Shrieker nests were moved into a picket formation around Great Britain.

Captain Pryce epitomized the ideal sentry dragon captain; cool, focused and unflappable, the ideal counterbalance to the impulsive, distractible species. The first priority of such a captain was to reign in her dragon's impetuous desire to attack the interlopers long enough to radio in the attackers' position and vectors, then hold off his aggression enough to remain a harassing presence for the enemy dragons without endangering her crew, until the intercepting flight of allied dragons arrived to drive the enemy off. To maintain such discipline required an intense mastery of her own passions, which she found to be most easily achieved by allowing her other passions utterly free reign on the ground.

The sight of Captain Pryce striding up to any aviator who caught her eye, directly and confidently telling the lucky aviator what she wanted to do to him (and what she expected of his performance in return) was a common one, and many aviators ached for an opportunity to earn her approval.

Opposite: Captain Helena Pryce, astride Lynceus, her Crested Shrieker

# Spitfire

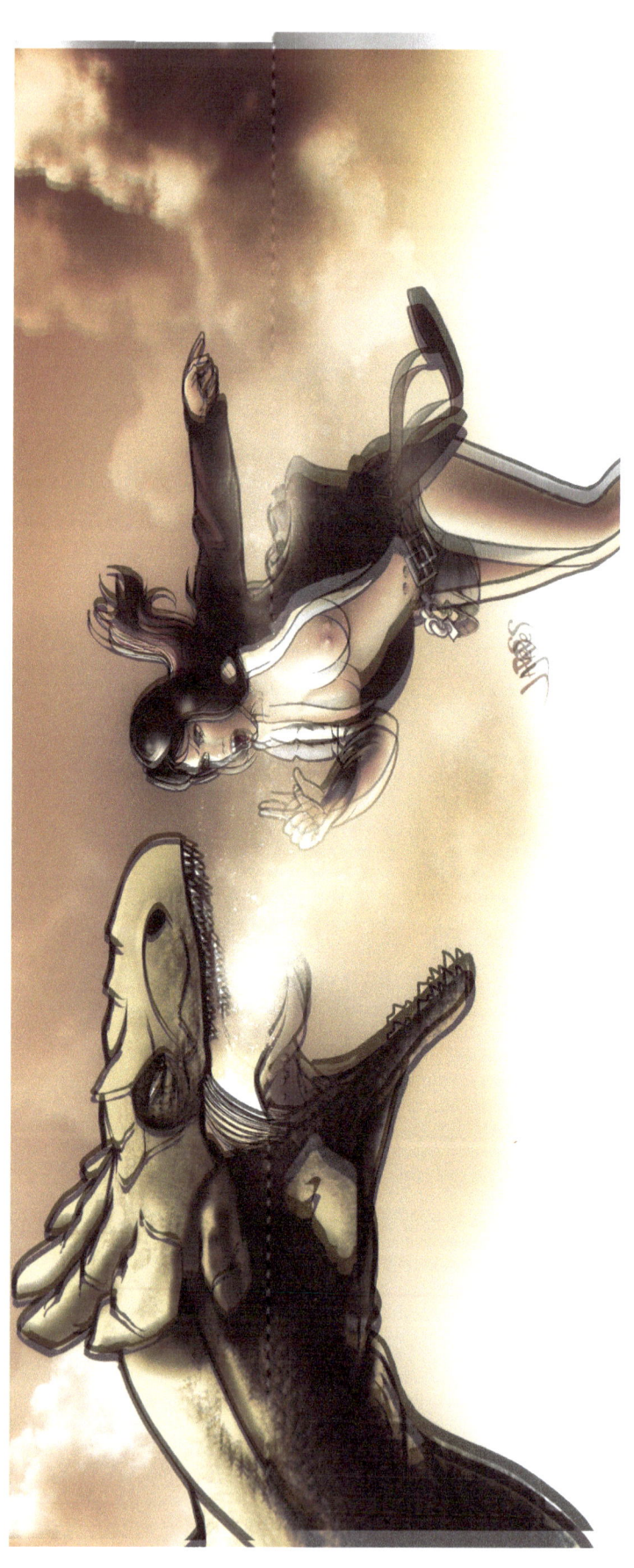

Dragons **never** attacked their crew, not even in the cases of documented harsh abuse. To the dragons, it would be the equivalent of destroying a priceless diamond that had cut you, even if they had not developed a deep attachment and affection for their captains. Nevertheless, in the pressure of wartime, oftentimes heated disagreements will break out between soldiers, and dragons were not immune to this, nor to the instinctual displays of aggression that flowed from frustration and wounded pride. Nevertheless, intellectually knowing your dragon won't harm you is a different beast altogether than staring down the maw of a five-tonne serpent as its displeasure with you manifests in a fiery glow roiling up its gullet. Thus, it took stark courage, and not a little fire of her own, for Captain Ashley Kalin (pictured) to dress down her Crested Scythewing, Horus.

# LET SLEEPING DRAGONS LIE

I was immensely gratified to see that my recruitment posters for the Corps had done their job and enticed hundreds of young men to join up, and try their luck with the nubile aviators I had drawn. Their numbers were sorely needed to fill out the ranks of the dragons' ground and air crews, which had been dwindling before the war, what with the fearsome reputations of dragons and the high casualty rates in the Corps (there were even widespread rumors linking the two-- that dragons were liable to eat crew members when hungry). Many of these hopeful young men, however, soon found their ardor diminished by the sight of the multi-tonne dragons and their protectiveness towards their crew, and became very shy to approach the very women they had enlisted to pursue.

Their fear was unjustified, however, as far from being sexually protective of their crew, dragons saw their crew breeding as a particular form of "wealth" and status. They were often heard boasting of the beauty of their female crew, hoping that the swelling in the recruits' groins would soon lead to a swelling in the ranks of their crew. Likewise, in the matter of actual mating, dragons often resembled nothing more than pushy would-be grandparents not-so-subtly encouraging a young couple to grant them grandchildren. Thus, the greatest threat to a would-be paramour was not so much to be engulfed by a dragon, as be embarrassed by one.

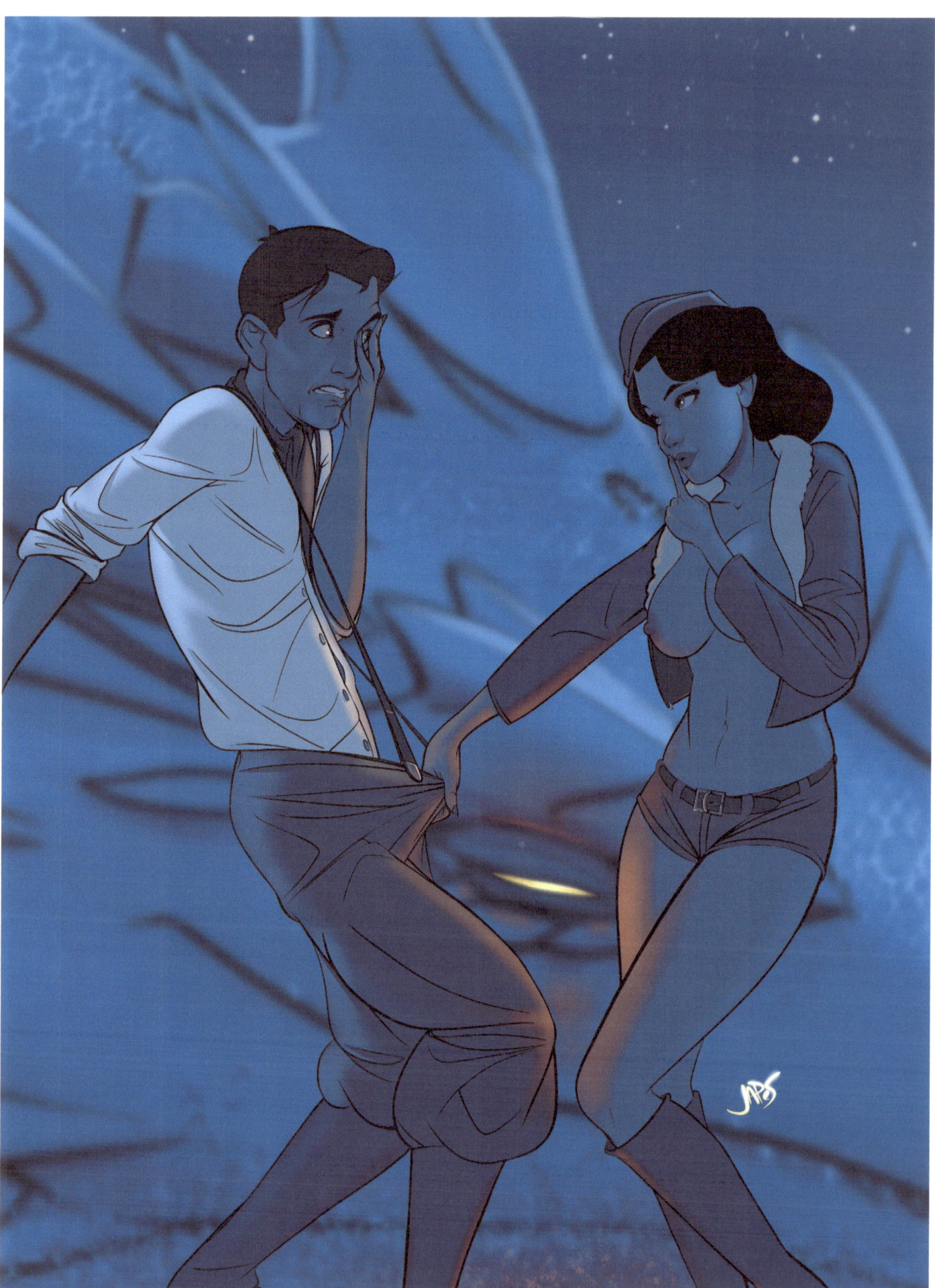

One night around the campfire, while trying to sleep, I overheard the booming "whispers" of Captain Alyxandra "Lyx" Moraine's dragon, Tarane, and Ravenscroft's Aurelius:

**Tarane**: Oy, Livingston, what are you doing with my captain? We're lifting off at 0500 and I don't want to hear any more complaining about--
**Aurelius**: Quiet, you! Can't you see they're making an egg?
**Tarane**: Oh! An egg! And about time, too! Ooh, ooh! Captain Moraine, can you make me a girl egg?
**Aurelius**: She can't do that.
**Tarane**: What do you mean, she can't? Young Livingston seems to be up for it, although his mast seems to be drooping, so to speak--
**Aurelius**: I mean, she can't choose the sex of the egg like we can, just by regulating our incubation temperature... they leave it up to chance.
**Tarane**: Well that's a right stupid way to do things, imagine-- hey! Oy, Livingston, just where do you think you're going? Livingston! Take those trousers off at once, get back in there and do your duty, good sir! LIVINGSTON!

Opposite: Captain Moraine, sneaking by her dragon, Tarane

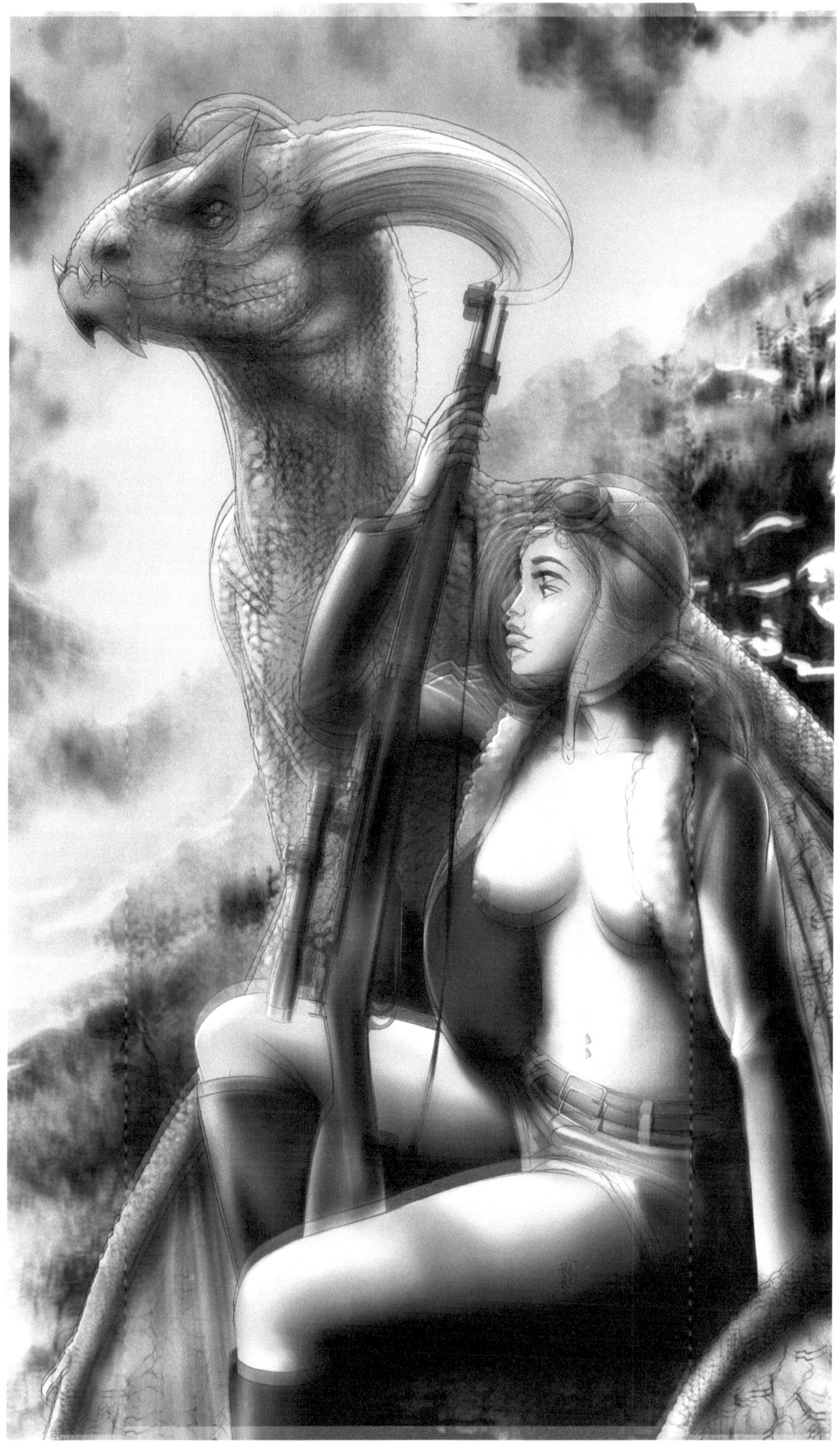

# Perfect Vision

Major Vanessa Hajek was sixteen when the Nazis rolled into her small village near the Stone Mountains; when relatives from nearby towns later found her people lying in a common grave and the village a smouldering ruin, she was feared dead. So the first surprise was when she came strolling down from the mountains a good three years later, taciturn and covered with scratches, but otherwise unharmed.

The second surprise was the dragon who descended the mountain with her-- Noir, a Mountain Gyrwyrm. A hardy and proud species, they scrupulously avoid humans, owing to centuries of villagers trying to exterminate them for making off with their sheep. Gyrwyrms, when not gliding high above on mountain thermals, are incredibly difficult to spot on the ground, owing to their limited, but still impressive, camouflage ability allowing them to blend incredibly well with their cliff side and rocky habitats. Face-to-face contact with one was a rarity, as they are likely, by both inclination and capability, to avoid humans altogether.

Nevertheless, the pair descended the mountain together-- the girl and her dragon companion, a serpentine shadow hissing at passers-by. No one ever found out whether the pair knew each other and somehow forged a bond before she escaped to the mountain, while she was guarding her family's flocks, or whether the dragon somehow took pity on the skinny orphan girl alone on the mountain and decided to adopt her. Noir tended to snarl at those brave enough to approach, and the girl wasn't much more welcoming of questions about her time in the wilderness.

Opposite: Mjr. Hajek with her Mountain Gyrwyrm, Noir

Eventually the pair made it to France, and then across the Channel to Britain, where they immediately volunteered for the British Commandos. Assigned to the 11th Special Air Service (SAS) Battalion, they were attached to Agamemnon's wing as assassins and saboteurs.

The duo were fierce, unyielding and frighteningly effective in their roles. While he was too small to actually carry her behind enemy lines, Noir was small enough to piggyback on a bomber dragon's back. And while not a powerful flyer, with long wings well-suited to gliding on updrafts rather than powerful beating, he did make an excellent modified parachute when she jumped at altitude while harnessed to him.

On the ground, Noir became a living sniper's nest and spotter combo, camouflaging her with his wing draped over her and using his incredible vision to call out targets and threats. For her part, Vanessa's childhood in the forests and fields of rural Czechoslovakia prepared her to be a peerless marksman, and her trauma instilled in her a seemingly unquenchable drive to kill Nazis. A shot echoing out from the direction of foothills or mountains, followed by the discovery of a dead Nazi officer, soon became known to announce the arrival of "The Wraith," as the duo became known, and signaled the start of days of terror for German officers, officials, and scientists.

So driven by bloodlust and so confident in their ability to avoid detection were the pair, that they usually lingered in the area after their primary target was eliminated, signaling for extraction only after the Major ran out of ammo.

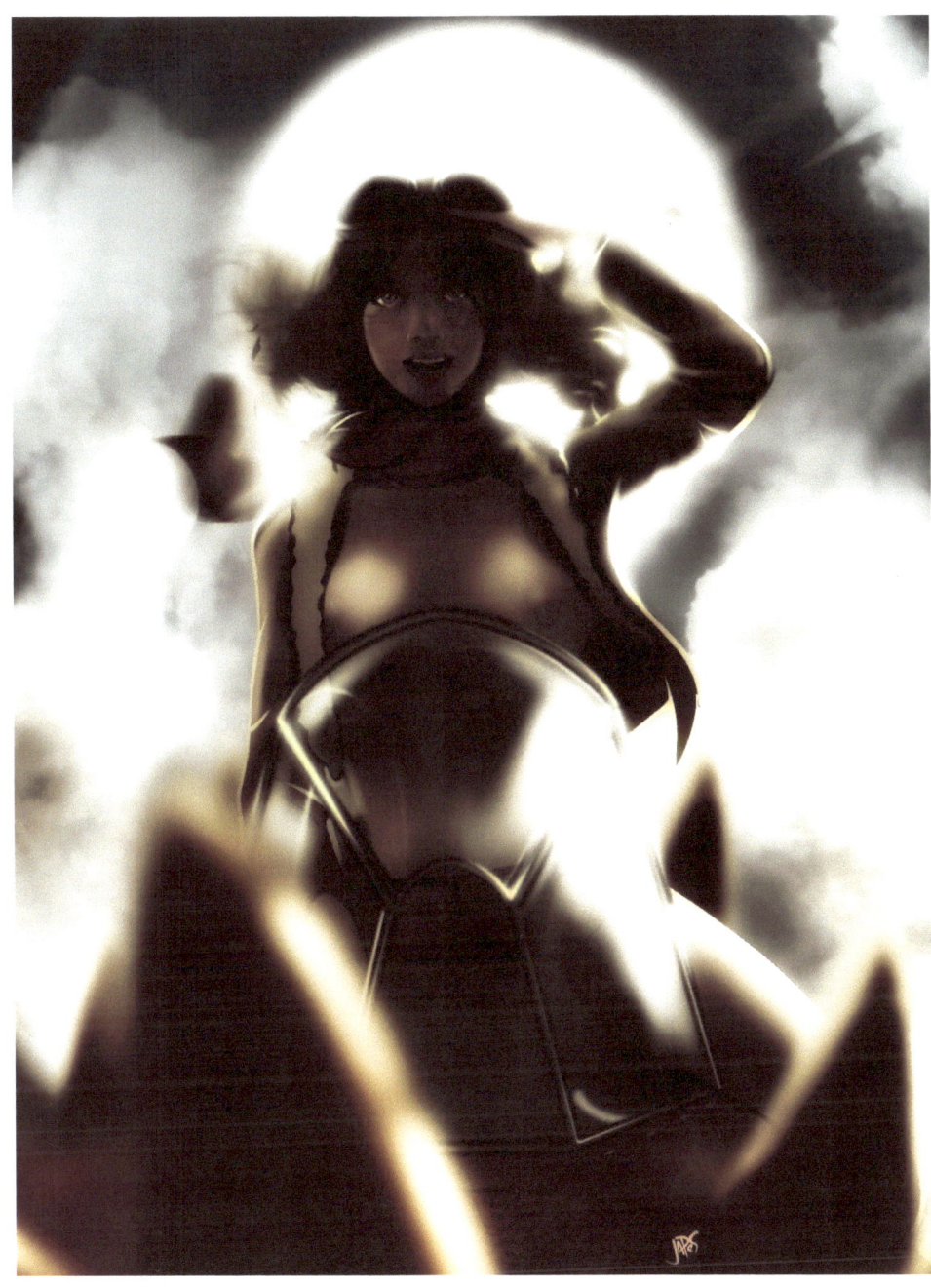

## STARING AT THE SUN

Captain Ophelia Henderson practices the time-honored battle technique of attacking from the direction of the sun. Although I painted this to be an alluring sight for our forces, I imagine this particular sight, in real combat, would have been the most terrifying thing to see. I always liked Capt. Henderson; never ostentatious, just steady and friendly, she was one of the first aviators I met when I came on base, and one of the last I got around to painting. Sadly, she was the only aviator whom I painted not to survive the war. She and her dragon Atalanta were lost in the skies above Dresden in '45.

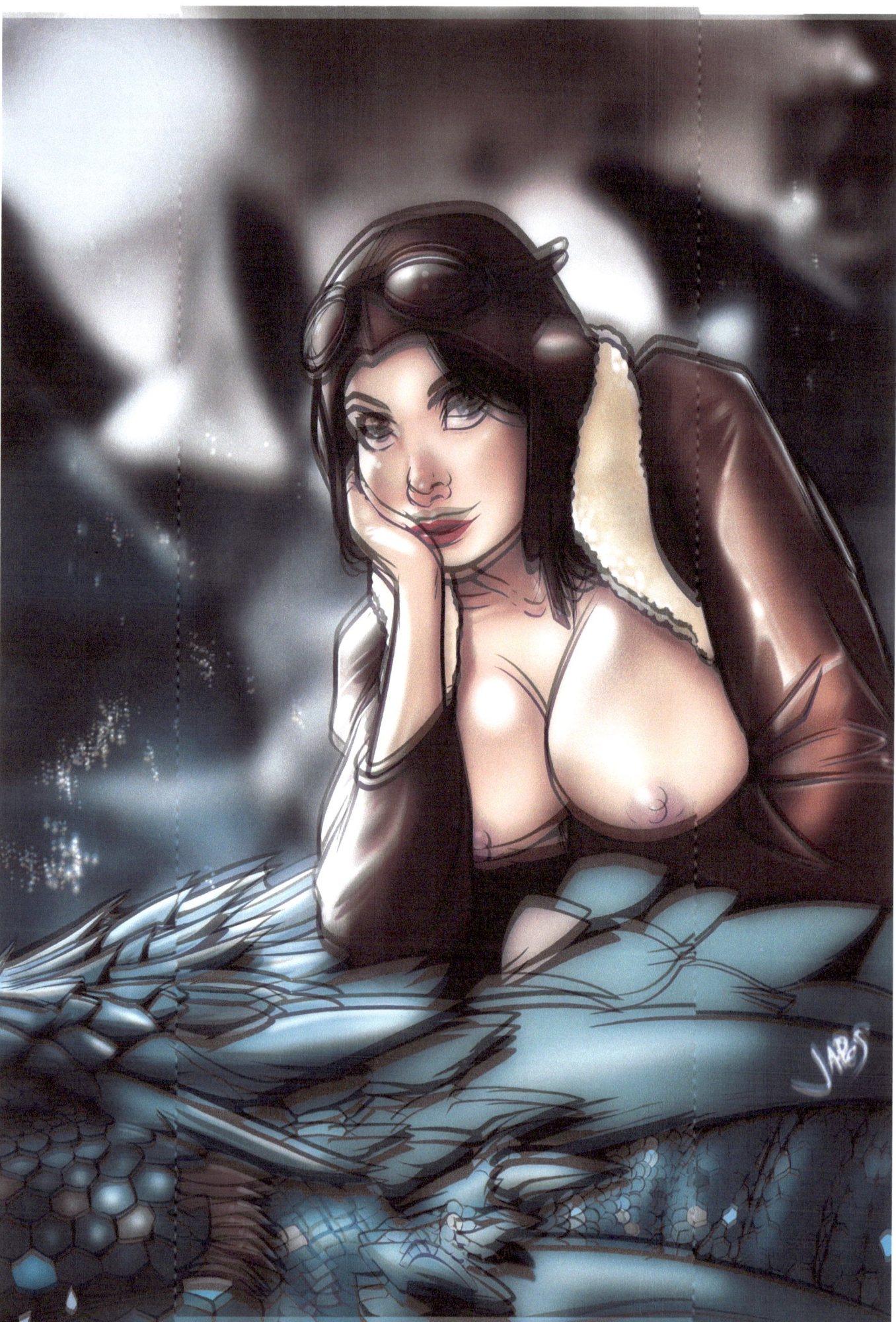

# MISSION DEBRIEF

Captain Amelia Watson leans on her Crowned Rook, Antilles, during a mission debriefing. In this study, I tried to capture that far-off look in her eyes as the tacticians and Admirals droned on about targets hit and the importance of ammo conservation.

I knew her well enough to know that while her body was grounded, her mind was lost in the clouds. Captain Watson was absolutely enthralled with the freedom of flying, and jumped at every chance to fly she could; she would have been one of the most decorated aviators in the Corps if she could have been persuaded to stay on the ground long enough to report her deeds. In this way, she was a perfect match for her Crowned Rook, as the breed were the champion long-distance flyers of dragons. Playful, clever, and easy-going, masters of navigating air currents and updrafts to conserve energy, and possessed of a fierce wanderlust, these dragons could stay aloft for days-- eating and even sleeping while airborne. In fact, Antilles was so-named because he once flew from Gibraltar to the island chain without claw touching ground.

Opposite: Captain Watson and Antilles

# AERIAL CORPS PRIDE

Flight Cadet Samantha Fox shows off her matching ink, with her dragon Ulysses. Dragons and aviators formed lifelong bonds, often codified by rituals such as getting matching tattoos. The dragons, their tattoos being drawn directly on their scales, never could figure out what the big deal was. Ulysses, in particular, said he would get a tattoo on every scale if he could, and was quite sure he didn't see what Cadet Fox was whinging on about.

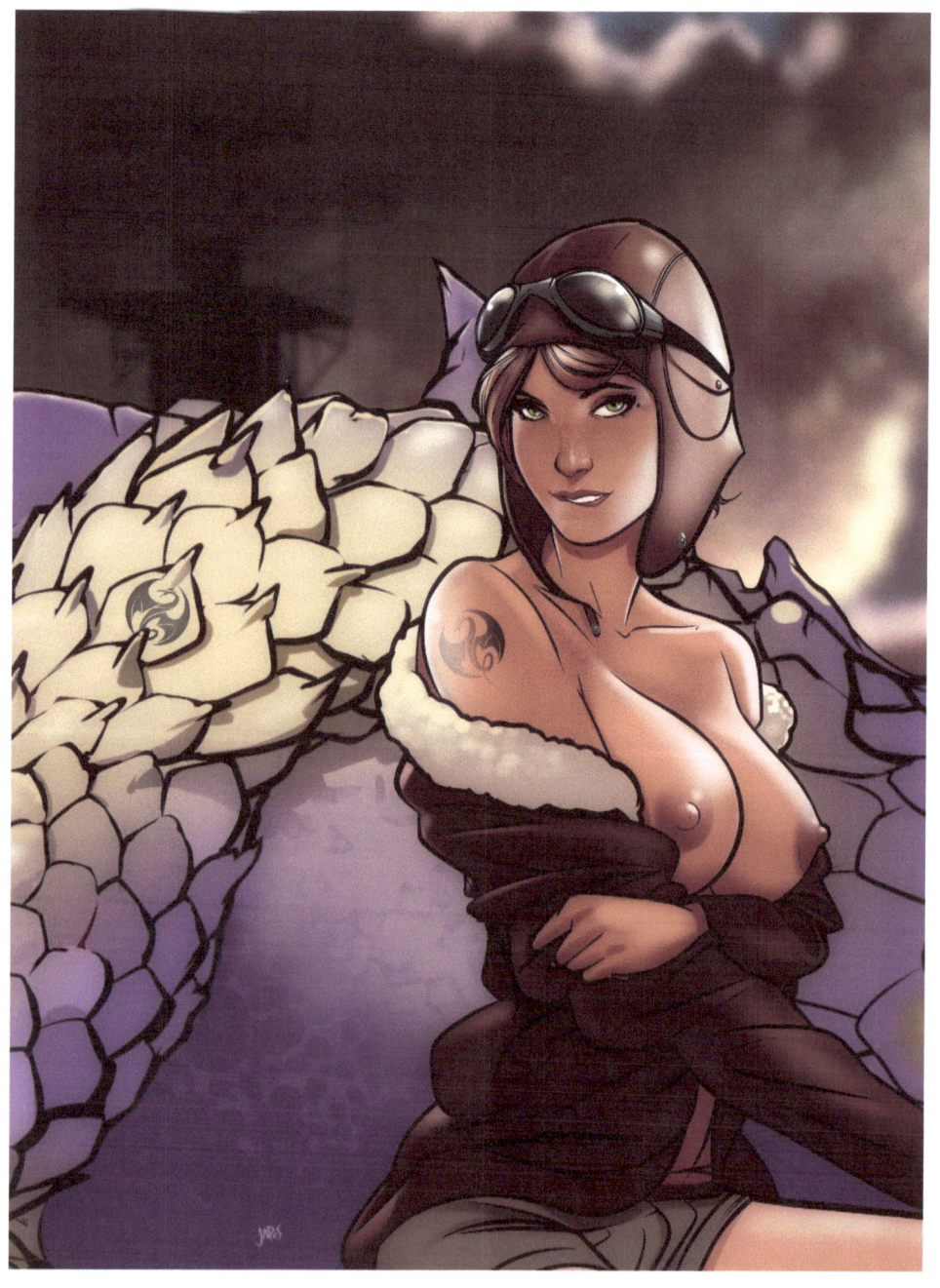

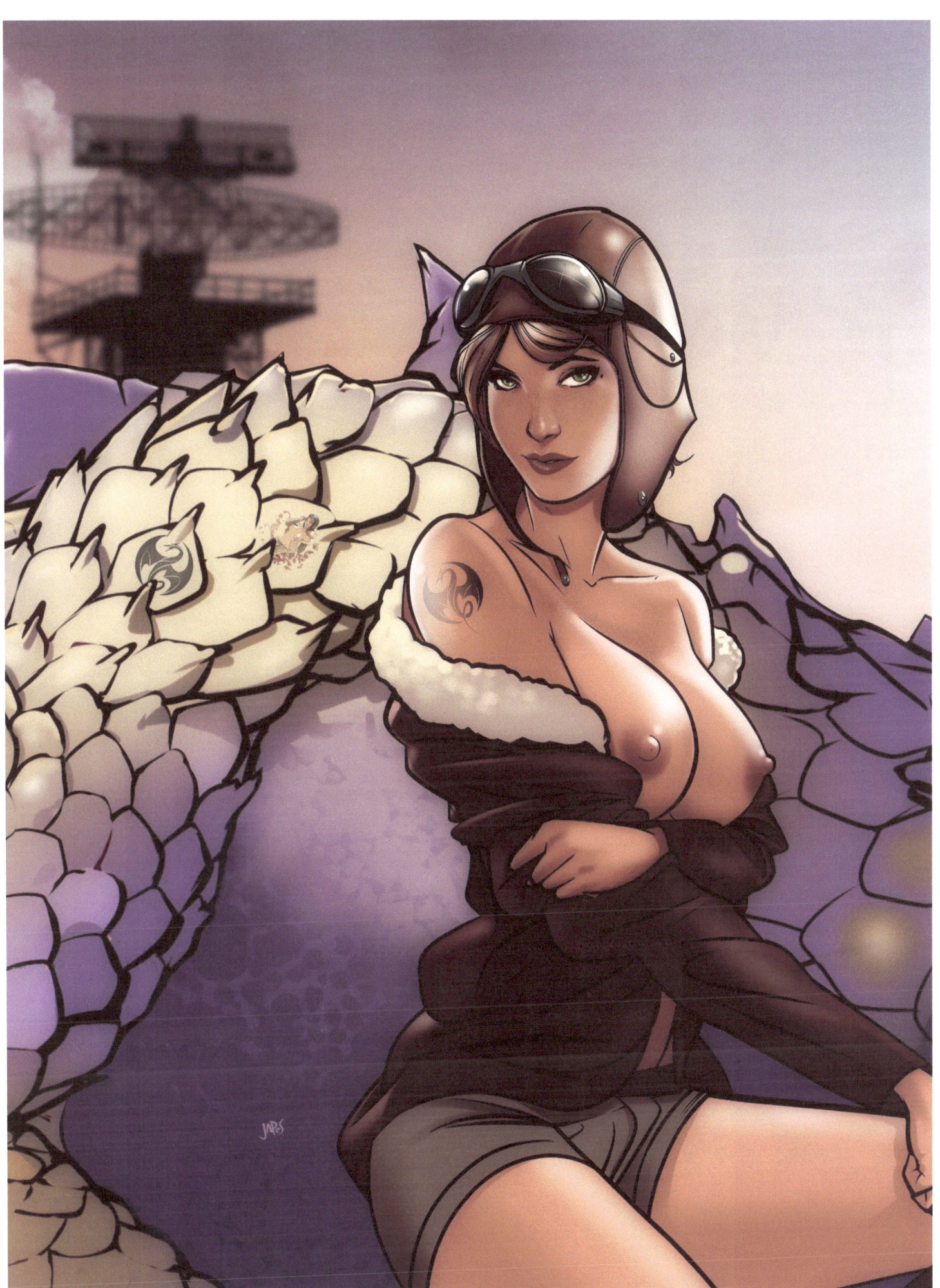

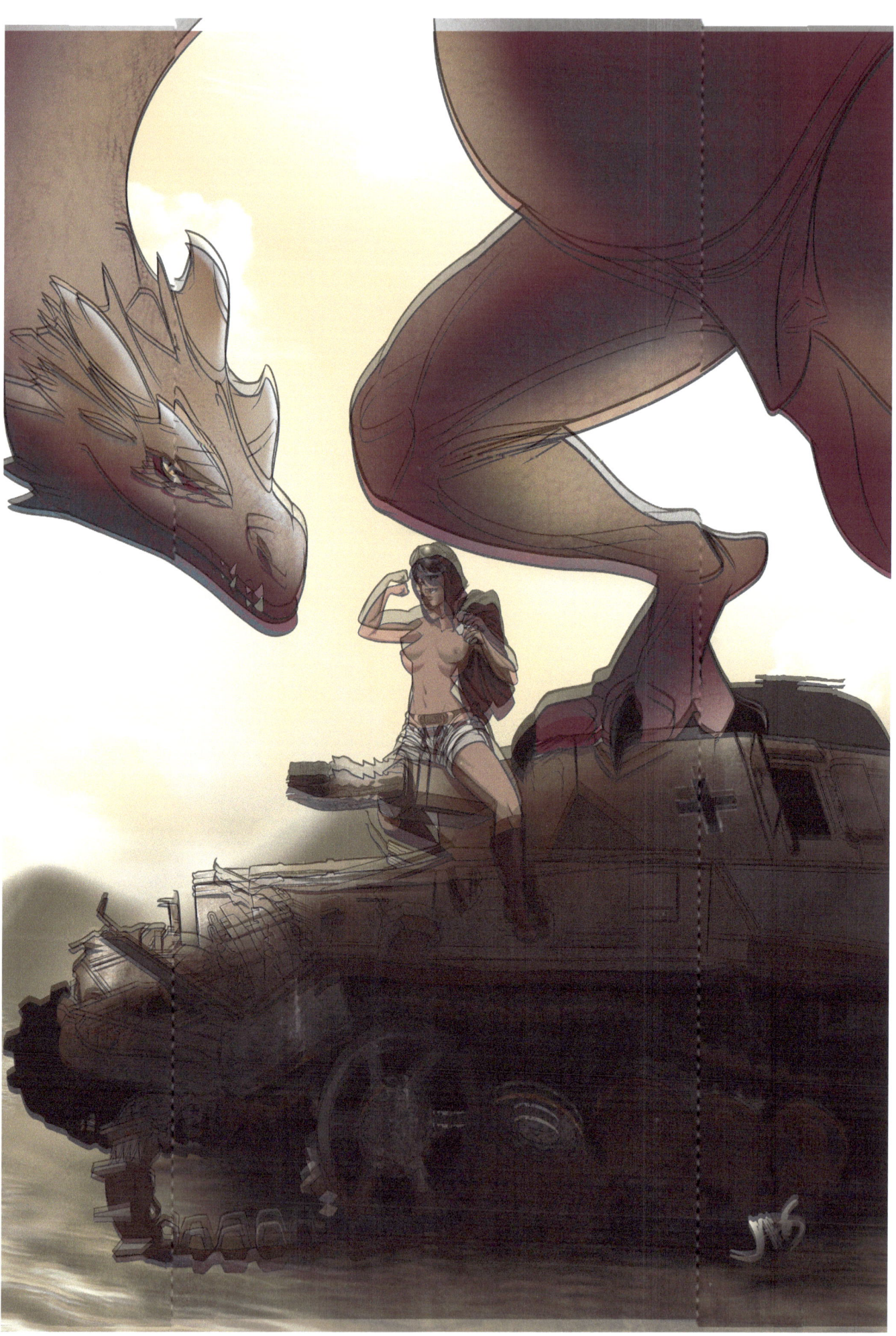

# Desert Fox

Dragons of the Corps proved instrumental in the eventual Allied victory in Tunisia, especially after coming to the rescue during the Second Battle of El Alamein. In fact, many of the dragons who took part in the fight boasted over and over that Rommel would not have enjoyed the success he had, had Field Marshal Montgomery not been so stubborn in keeping them out of the fray until then. In fact, "Old Monty," as they called him, had believed dragon power to be obsolete in the face of mechanized armor, and rebuffed multiple attempts from the Air Marshal to assist in the theatre. It was only in the face of sustained British tank losses that he relented, then watched in amazement as the dragons utterly destroyed the German tank army in a matter of minutes.

While he was correct that medium-weight dragons like Ramses could not penetrate the thick Panzer armor, and were in fact quite vulnerable to their shells, he had underestimated the degree of heat in the dragons' blue flames, which turned the tanks of the Afrika Korps into, as Ramses put it, "Dutch ovens on treads."

Captain Singh, full of pride after an early life filled with being underestimated due to her sex, race and caste, hardly bothered to put a damper on her dragon's exuberance. She herself had been rescued from a life of lower-caste servitude in India when her master, a British officer, died of malaria. Ramses, while incubating in the egg in the officer's care, had heard her singing daily while she worked, and upon hatching, refused to leave her for the Captain he was promised to. Long-believing she was worth more than she had been told, she blossomed with this validation.

Opposite: Captain Amari Singh and her Crowned Rukh, Ramses, say, "Rommel who?" as they pose with their Panzer trophy in North Africa.

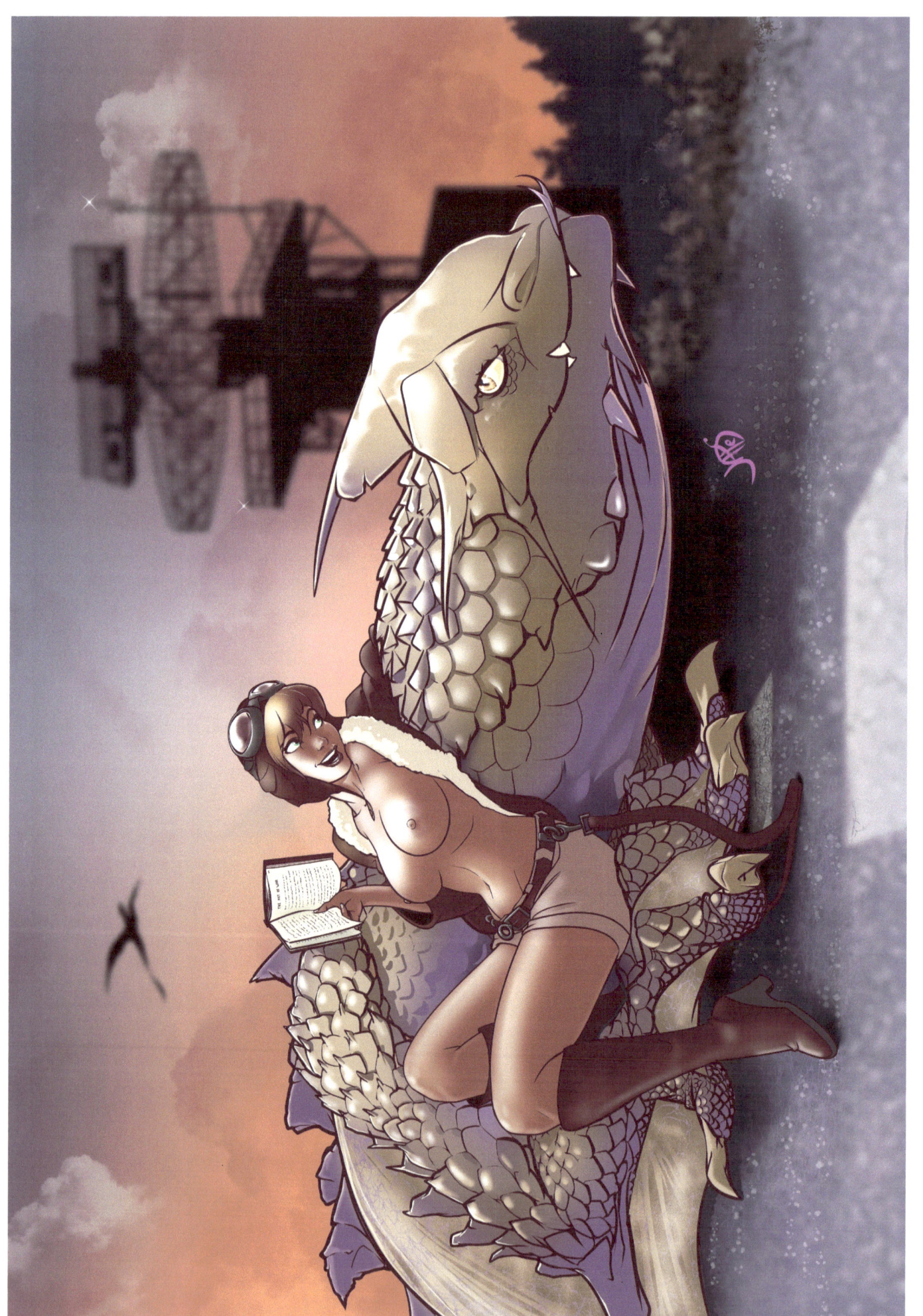

Captain Gwendolyn Andrews reads Sun Tzu's "The Art of War" to her Bullheaded Wyvern, Artemis.

# THE ART OF WAR

Named for their distinctive rounded heads, and not (as commonly assumed) for their temperaments, Bullheaded Wyverns are in fact flexible, free-thinkers, fond of philosophy and voracious learners. As with other dragon species, Bullheads start absorbing ambient language while still in the egg, and by the time they are hatched, are ready for Mark Twain-level literature. Young dragons tend to be especially demanding of their captains, who spend much of their down time reading entire libraries-worth of books to their dragons.

As intelligent as they are, neither do their bulbous skulls house particularly larger brains; their distinctive shapes instead house a labyrinthine series of sinuses that act as resonance chambers, amplifying their roars to a pitch and volume that overloads and shuts down the nervous systems of their targets. This supremely powerful weapon nevertheless has a relatively short range, necessitating their role as "flying tanks," offering low-altitude infantry support on the battlefield.

Flying so low exposed the Bullheads to heavy ground fire; though the heavily armored and swift-flying species was largely impervious to small-arms fire, their captains were not. Thus, they tended to guard their captains especially jealously. None more so than Artemis with Captain Andrews; she insisted that the charming, expressive, lively and beautiful young aviator sleep with her every night, and not just for the bedtime stories.

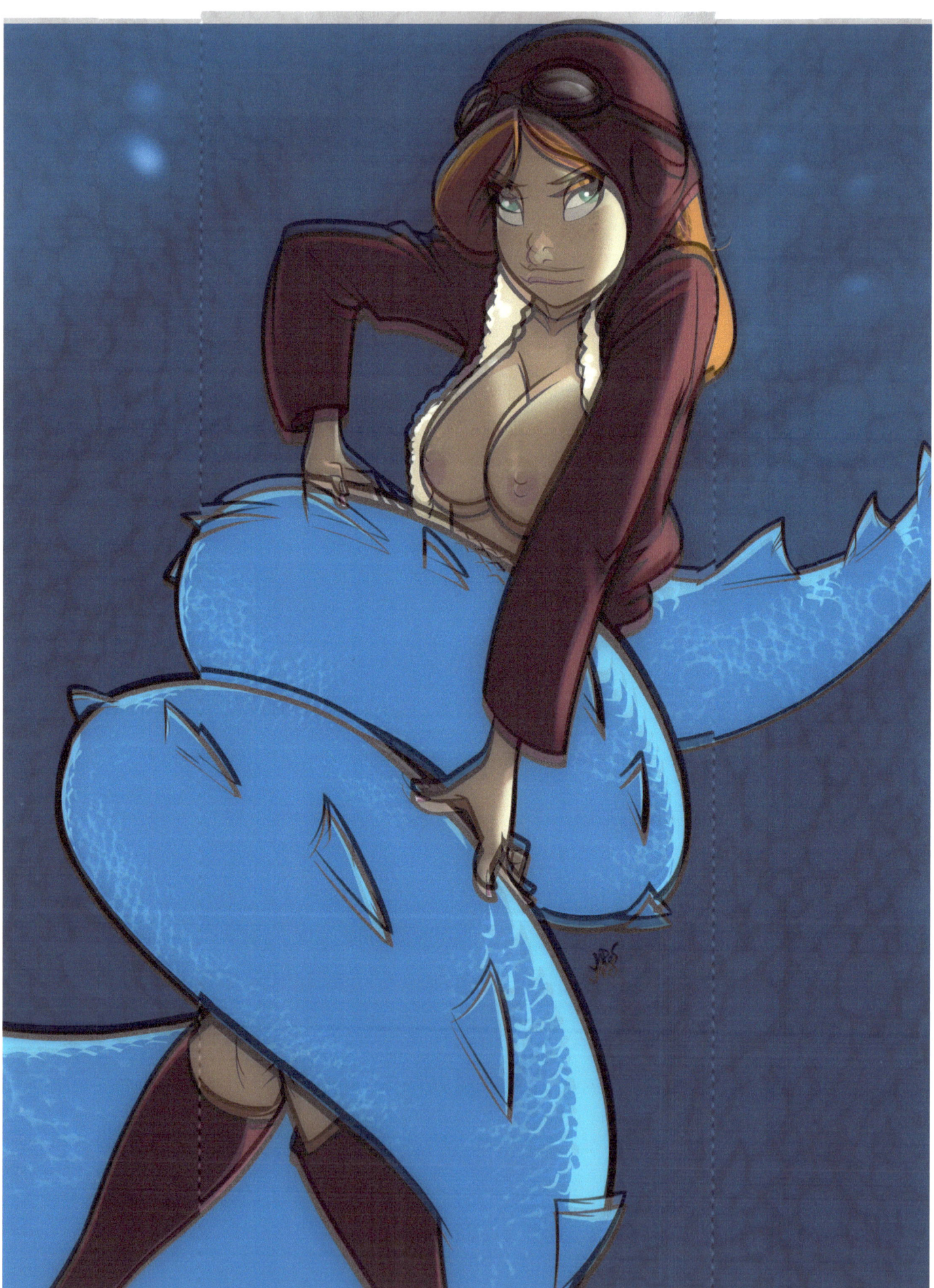

# Overprotective

As the major determinant of dragon status in the Corps was the size and beauty of one's crew, dragons tended to treat their more attractive female crew as particularly precious jewels. To the dragons' way of thinking, a beautiful female crew would attract more male crew members eager to seek a mate, and thus swell a dragon's ranks. Plus, the more attractive breeding females, the more chance of children which would become attached to long-lived dragons in the next generation. In fact, many dragons became amateur experts in "human husbandry," studying and appraising their crew for signs of health and fertility like large breasts, wide hips, and so on. While ensuring dragon loyalty and interest in the outcome of the war, the dragons' predilection for viewing their female crew as valuable "collectibles" had the distressing side effect of dragons sometimes becoming overprotective of some of their crew when fighting. Some dragons developed the distressing habit of coiling themselves protectively around aviators in the midst of a firefight, sometimes spoiling their shot and often limiting their combat effectiveness. In rare cases, dragons were even known to grab their crew and beat a hasty retreat, if they felt their prized women overly threatened, abandoning their comrades in the midst of a battle. Given that once this happened, the Corps would respond by forcibly reassigning the crew of the jealous dragon, dragon captains were constantly trying to stamp out any signs of dragon overprotectiveness.

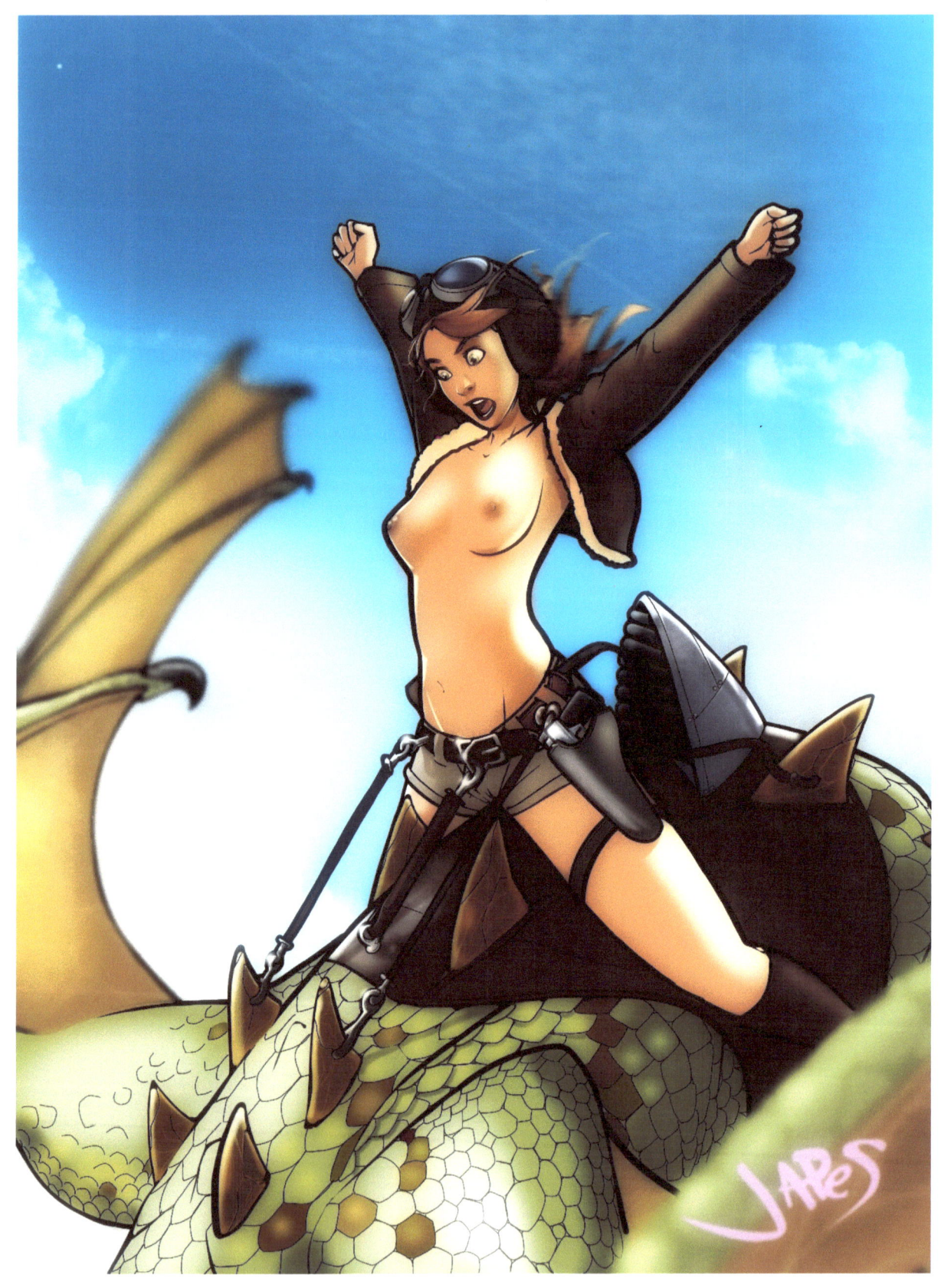

Lt.McTiernan with Brutus

# First Flight

Despite their names, Copper Spitfires did not breathe fire, but rather spat a strong acid capable of burning through wing membranes and blinding enemy dragons.

Natural pack hunters, these small, agile dragons proved a perfect fit for patrol missions during the Battle of Britain, eventually turning the tide and repelling enemy bombers from the skies over the Kingdom. Bonding just one human pilot with the pack leader gained the allegiance and attack capability of the entire pack, which would converge on the Alpha's target and bring the enemy down in a swarm of slashing, spitting and biting.

The use of natural pack hunters enabled maximum attack coordination and dragon numbers while minimizing the need for trained human riders, which were at a premium at this phase of the war. This came with a significant downside, however, as pack leaders were (as a consequence of having to constantly fend off challenges to their status from ambitious pack members) generally spiteful, quick to react to perceived slights, suspicious and resistant to authority from their superiors. This limited their utility in the war to a largely defensive role, well-suited to patrolling and defending their territory, but generally unable to maintain the discipline and coordination needed to execute offensive strikes. The necessary decision to only bond riders with pack alphas also tended to reinforce the natural dragon tendency to view their human riders as treasures and symbols of status, and pilots had to be careful not to inadvertently instigate bloody power struggles (by showing favor to the wrong dragon) nor to not grow overly attached to any one dragon, as weak or wounded dragons tended to be rather ruthlessly dispatched in the maintenance of pack hierarchy. It was thus a testament to Brutus's strength, as well as Lieutenant McTiernan's flying and diplomatic skills, that she remained his rider for a majority of the war.

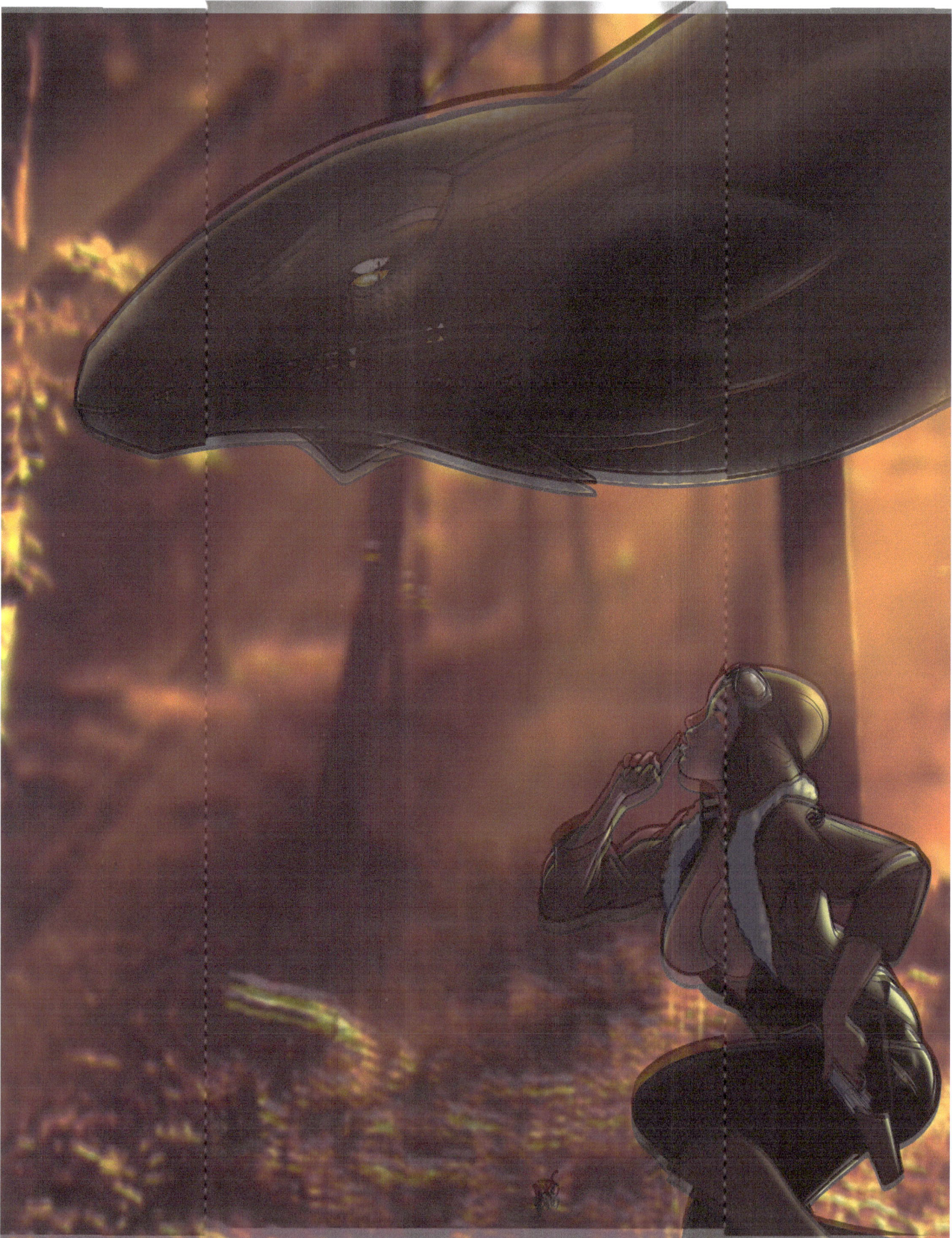

# STEALTH BOMBER

Captain Emma Coleman and her Bearded Wraith, Nix, sneak through the Ardennes Forest, behind enemy lines. Though "sneaking" for a dragon on the ground usually means knocking over a minimum of trees, and footsteps only sounding like distant thunder, Captain Coleman and Nix were the paragons of stealth while airborne.

As part of the elite "Black Cats" commando unit (so named because when they crossed an enemy's path, that enemy was very unlucky indeed), Captain Coleman and Nix were nigh-undetectable at night, where Nix's acid spitting and envenomed bite made the duo ideal assassins and saboteurs. The Black Cats had a foreboding reputation among other aviators, and Captain Coleman's background was, admittedly, another barrier to her full acceptance in the Corps. Hailing from the British Colony of Anglo-Egyptian Sudan, she was an accidental pilot, as typically "Colonials" were not allowed the privilege of piloting dragons. But when Nix hatched prematurely in the colony and imprinted on her for life, the Corps could ill-afford to mothball such a valuable dragon over such provincial concerns. Captain Coleman was quiet and reserved to strangers, but had a wide, easy smile and displayed a raunchy sense of humour to those who got to know her. And once enemy defenses failed to respond and bridges collapsed due to her advance work, she found herself the subject of many a toast and invitation to drinks at the pub from those eager to do just that.

Opposite: Captain Coleman and Nix

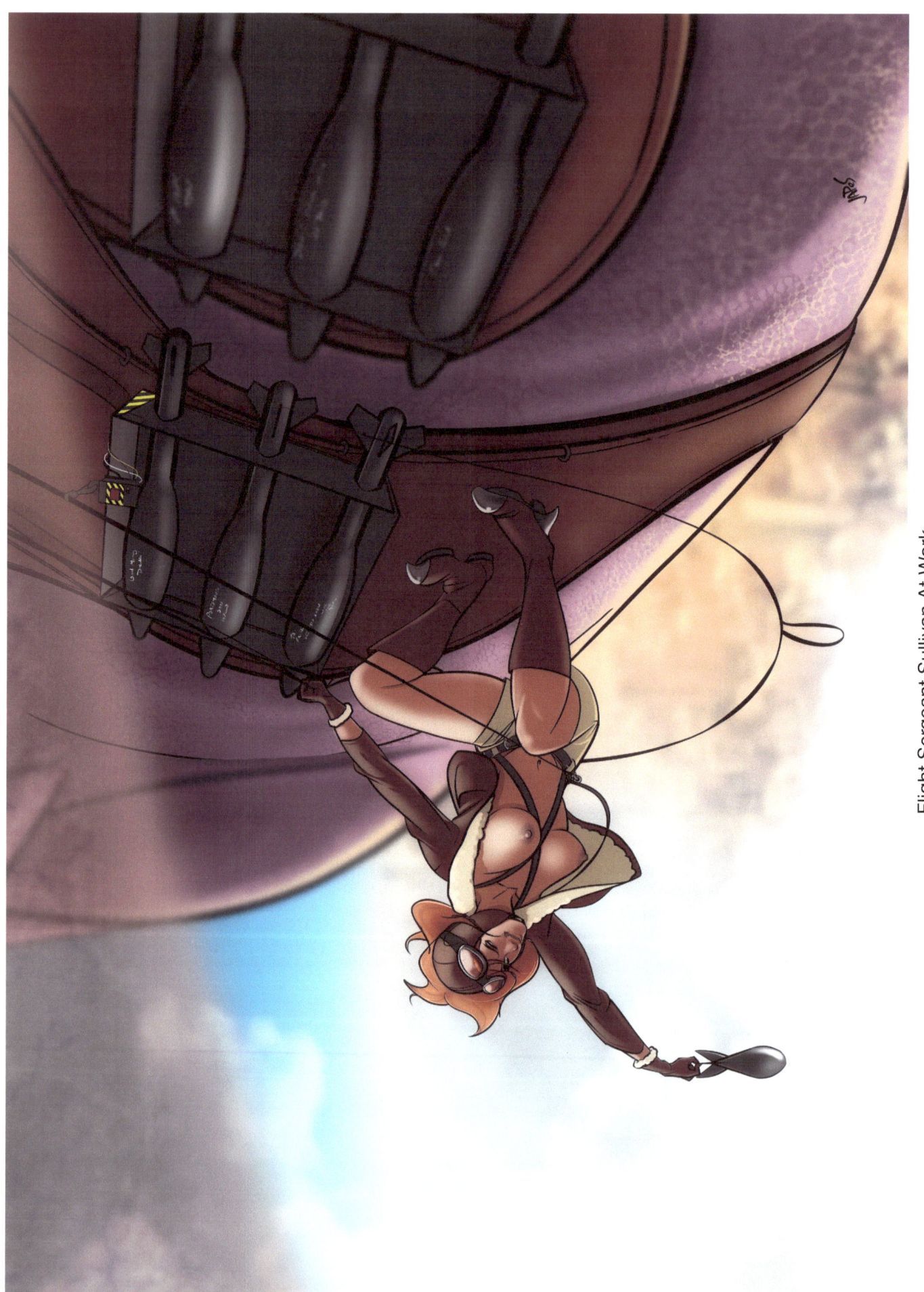

Flight Sergeant Sullivan At Work

# BOMBARDIER

The bombardier was the athlete of a dragon's crew, expected to have the acrobatic grace of a gymnast, the strength of a wrestler, and the aim of an expert marksman, as she clambered and swung over a dragon's flanks. Here, Flight Sergeant Bronwyn Sullivan takes aim with a tracer bomb, which was designed to leave a bright smoke trail upon release and explode with a bright flash. She would then, marking its path, adjust her bomber dragon's hovering position and then unleash the full payload on the unfortunate target.

Due to their flexibility, dexterity, and courage, the lovemaking skills of Bombardiers became the stuff of legend and innuendo among much of the Corps, and they became much sought-after mating partners among the enlisted men. In reality, they were no better between the sheets than any of their comrades, as gymnastic skills proved to not be quite the difference-maker some had hoped.

I once was witness to a young Private, Gerald Seinfeld, remarking that her performance was, "disappointingly pedestrian," after a dalliance with Sergeant Sullivan. Her dragon, overhearing, roundly thrashed the airman, remarking that he would be well-served not to attempt any future comedy within the dragon's earshot.

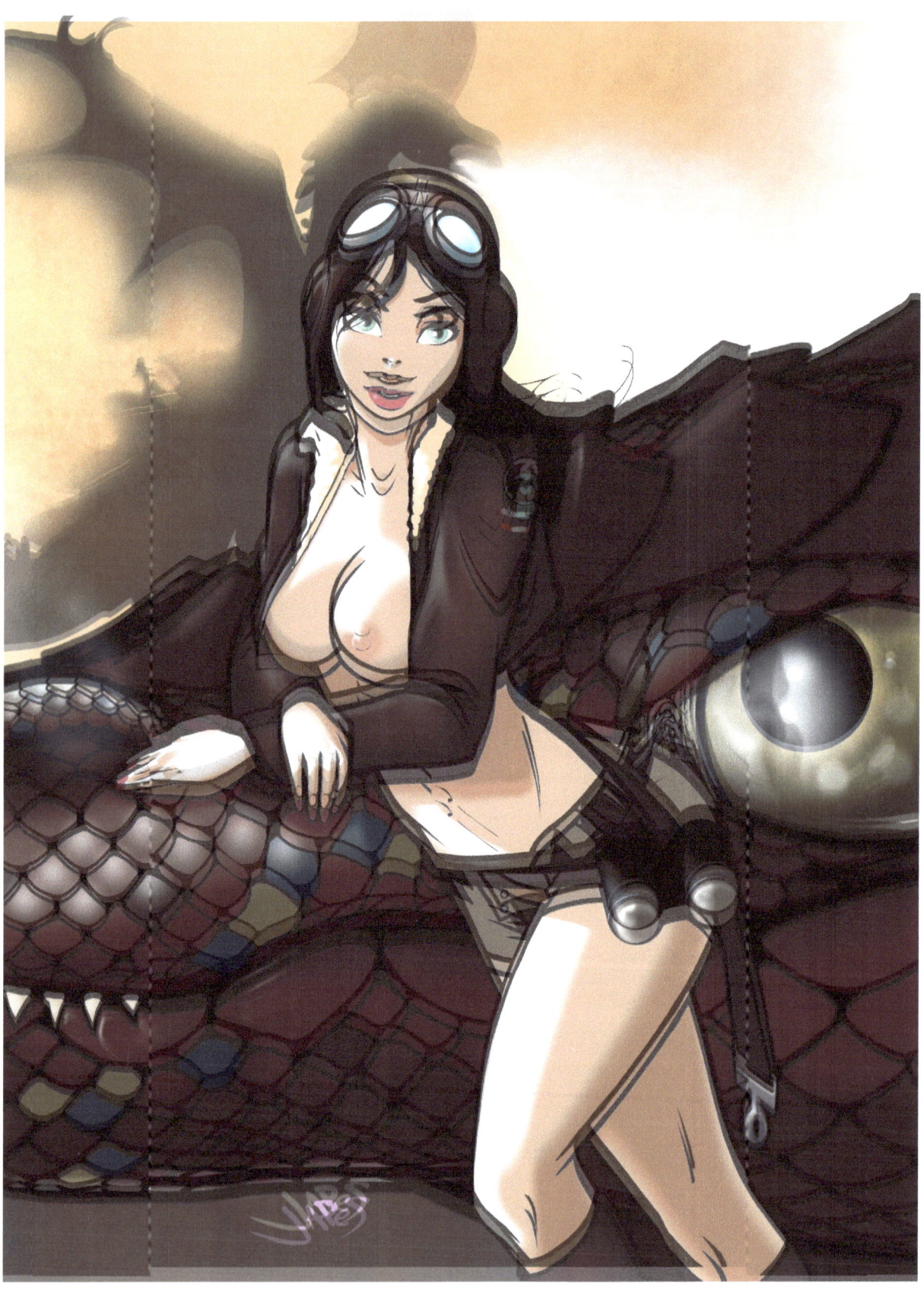

# Our Eyes In The Skies

A Crimson Reaper, one of the few dragon breeds known to prey on other dragons in the wild, Aurelius nonetheless remained a trusted part of Agamemnon's wing for the duration of the war. An excellent all-purpose fighter, and a fierce and wily warrior, Aurelius was an excellent example of the benefits of having reapers in a bomber group, regardless of the wariness they might have inspired in some of their squadron mates. The species' keen eyesight and ability to glide for long distances made them excellent at reconnaissance missions, with Captain Ravenscroft and Aurelius flying off ahead of the group to scout on targets, then circling back to report on ground and air defenses. Once debriefed, Captain Ravenscroft would then steer Aurelius to higher altitudes, where they would prove to be the key reason Agamemnon's group never lost a dragon to enemy fliers. As a high-altitude shadow to the bombing wing, Ravenscroft deployed Aurelius' hunting skills to devastating effect. His devastating momentum in a dive-bomb, together with powerful talons, proved an instant kill against smaller enemy dragons, while an envenomed bite finished off any larger dragons. Over the course of the war, Agamemnon's fear of having the dragons' apex predator in his wing gave way to a deep and lasting friendship, as he began to rely on the older dragon's sage counsel. The friendship was first tested, then strengthened, by his losing Jessica Ravenscroft, Captain Aubrey's second-in-command and one of the jewels of his flight crew, to Aurelius when she was promoted to Captain her own dragon. But Agamemnon quickly overcame that initial jealousy. Soon, Aurelius and Agamemnon could be heard conspiring nightly about which male member of Agamemnon's crew could be bred with Jessica, and which dragon would take possession of the resulting offspring; a topic which was a source of embarrassment, entertainment, and excitement to the human crews, as dragons are terrible at whispering quietly.

Opposite: Captain Jessica Ravenscroft, with her dragon Aurelius

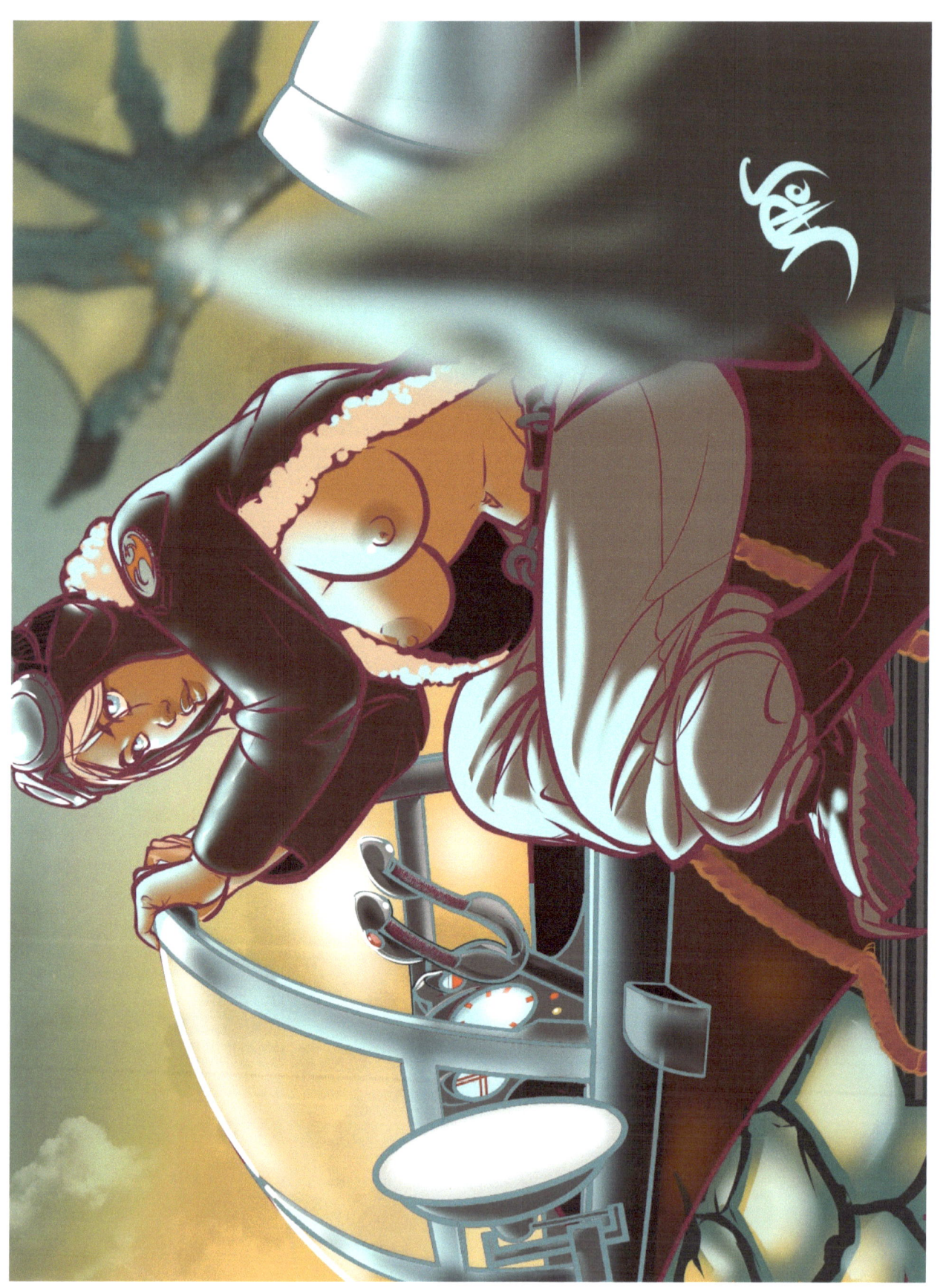

Captain Penny Maturin and her Royal Copper, Ajax, ready for a pre-dawn raid.

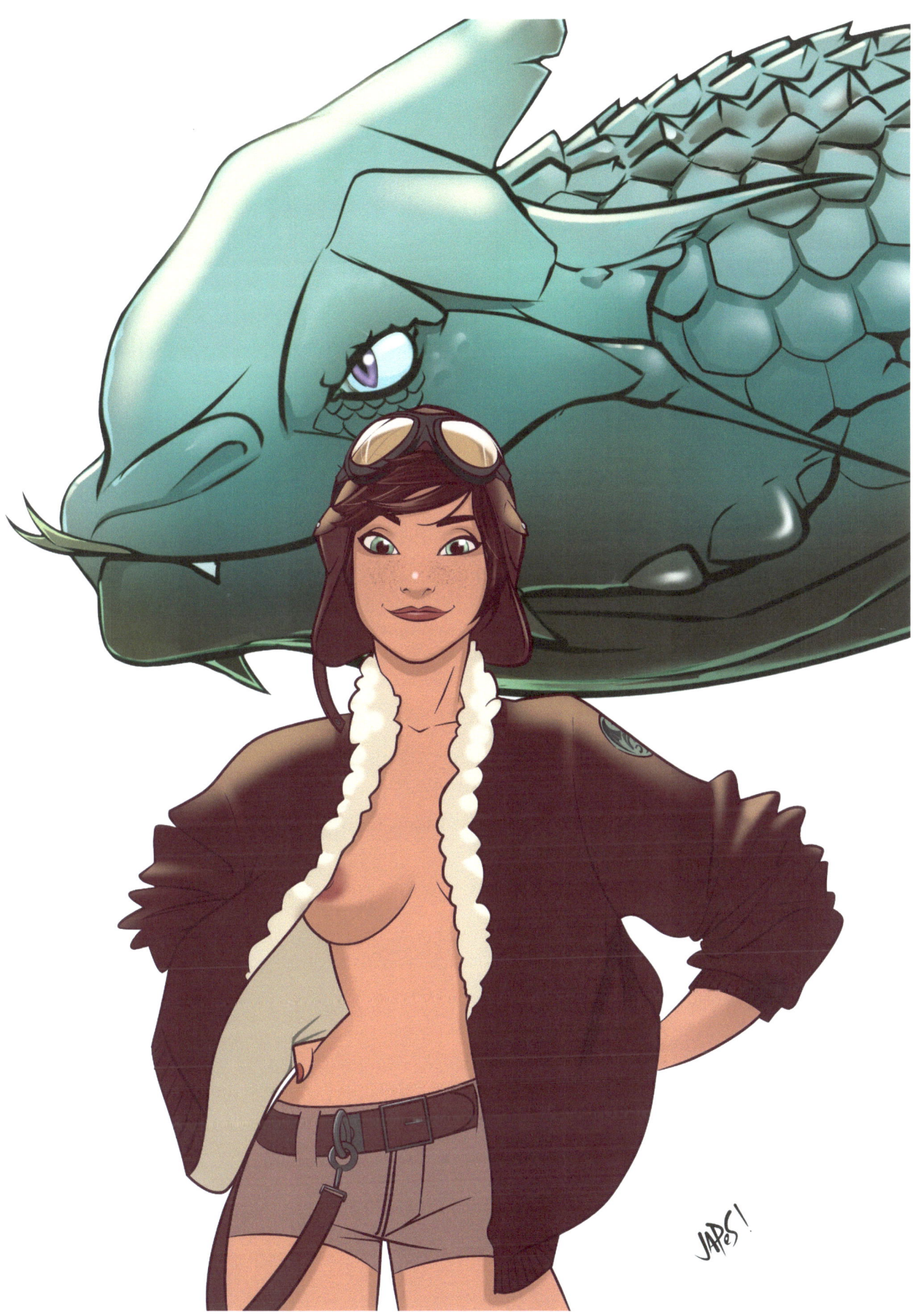

Flight Lieutenant Meredith "Brownie" Brown poses next to her Bull Fisher dragon, Thalassa

# MOXIE

Bull Fishers are larger, ocean-faring relatives of Bullheaded Wyverns, and primarily prey on Krakens, though they occasionally feast on giant squid, smaller whales, whale sharks, mantas and sunfish when their preferred prey are hard to come by. Putting their natural skills to use as Kraken hunters, they protected Allied shipping lanes from sea monster attacks and decimated the German Kraken Navy.

For this picture, I tried to convey the pride that these remarkable women took in their dragons, and in their part in the war effort. Liberated from the shackles of "polite society," they came into their own as a fierce, determined and loyal fighting force. Were it not for their efforts, the war would have been lost, and they knew it. History shows that having tasted liberation in the Corps, they continued to exhibit their love of freedom and their can-do spirit in the post-war period, as the free world rebuilt and awoke to a new age.

I was truly fortunate to live among them, to witness their humour, warmth, determination, bravery, grief, sacrifice and honor, and to use my art to show the world what the spirit of the Royal Dragon Corps was all about. I'll admit I overplayed the sexiness angle a bit-- though they really were quite sexually liberated and quite frequently half-dressed while at leisure, critics are right that riding a dragon at altitude while topless would result in one's naughty bits being frozen off. But as Air Marshall Lane put it, rather indelicately, "We need recruits to win this war, and nothing brings them in like tits."

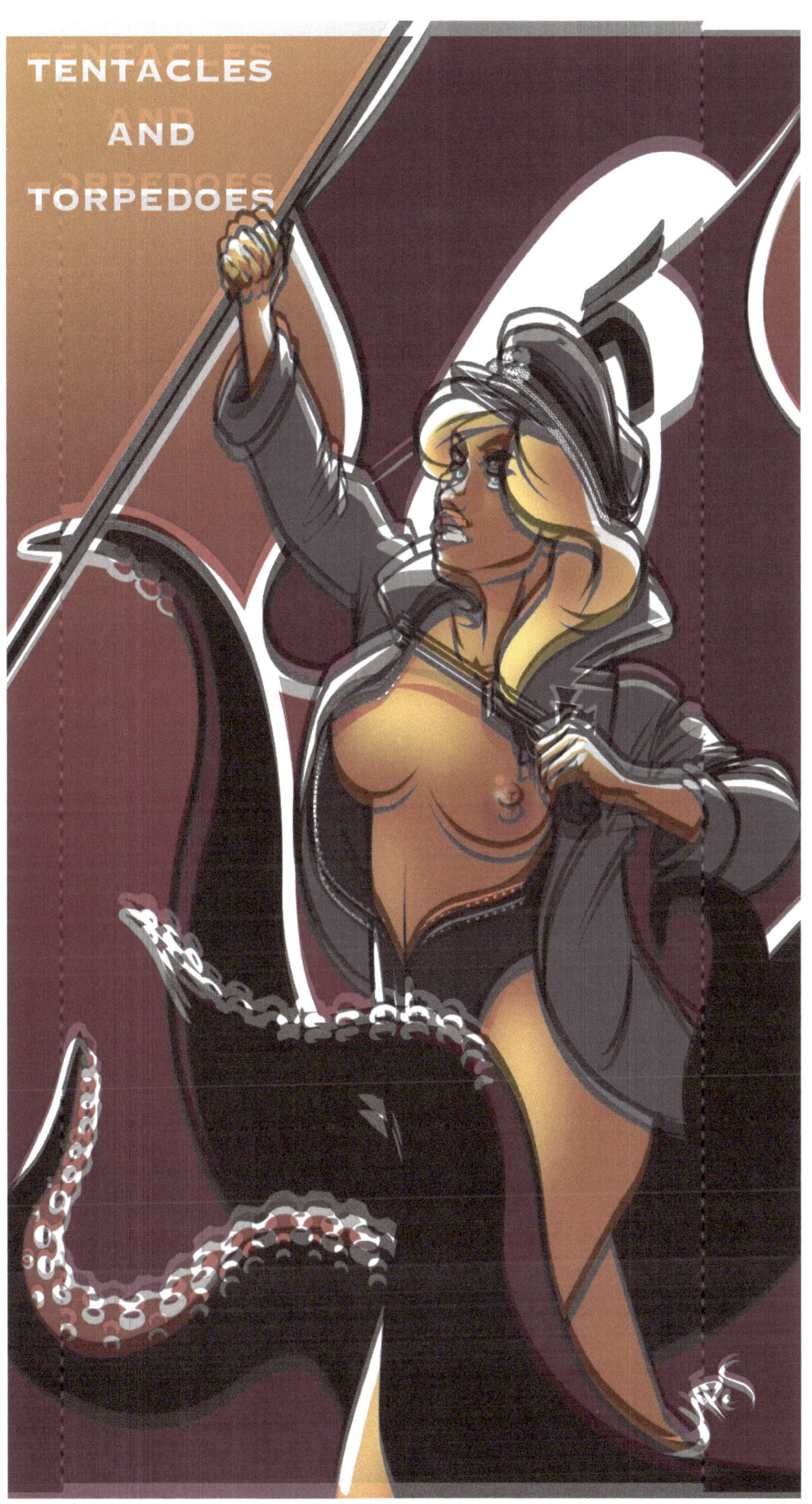

# Tentacles and Torpedoes: The German Kraken Fleet During WW2

From the author of "Scales and Chrome: Aerial Dragon Combat In the Second Great War" comes, "Torpedoes and Tentacles: The German Kraken Fleet in World War II."

"Feeling the tide of the war turning once the British beat back the Axis dragons in the Battle of Britain, and with air superiority slipping away in the face of the wildly successful Allied dragon breeding program, the Third Reich turned to an unholy alliance with a race of creatures long believed to be legend.

Nazi scientists, finally finding some success in their mining the realms of the occult for superweapons, not only managed to find the mythic behemoths of the deep, but also communicate with them well enough to enter into a Faustian bargain.

And so, with the resurrection of the ancient practice of chaining virgins to seaside cliffs as a sacrifice to the Kraken, the Nazis ensured the aid of the sea creatures in terrorizing Allied shipping lanes and sending many an Allied convoy to the depths. But unlike in ancient times, when the virgin sacrifices were quickly devoured, these young German women were allowed, for a while, to serve as the Kraken's "captain" and crew, until such time as the creature's appetites could no longer be denied. Living in airtight metallic quarters fused with the Krakens' monstrous flesh, life for these Krakenschiffers was often nasty, brutish, and short, each day a delicate dance of patiently enduring the creatures' baser appetites while attempting to relay orders from Naval Command and direct the creatures' bloodlust against appropriate Allied targets, knowing all the while that the tiniest slight would often be enough to hasten their ignominious doom.

Thus, with a steady stream of sacrifices needed to maintain the Krakens' aid, and with an increasingly suspicious public uneasy at the need for so many of their daughters to leave on such long tours at sea, German propaganda artists became instrumental in the maintenance of German naval superiority. Portraying the Krakenschiffers as fearless (and nubile) defenders of the Fatherland, at the helm of monstrously powerful creatures that would make their enemies quail in fear, these master artists even managed the impressive feat of ensuring that a significant minority of Kraken sacrifices were volunteers."

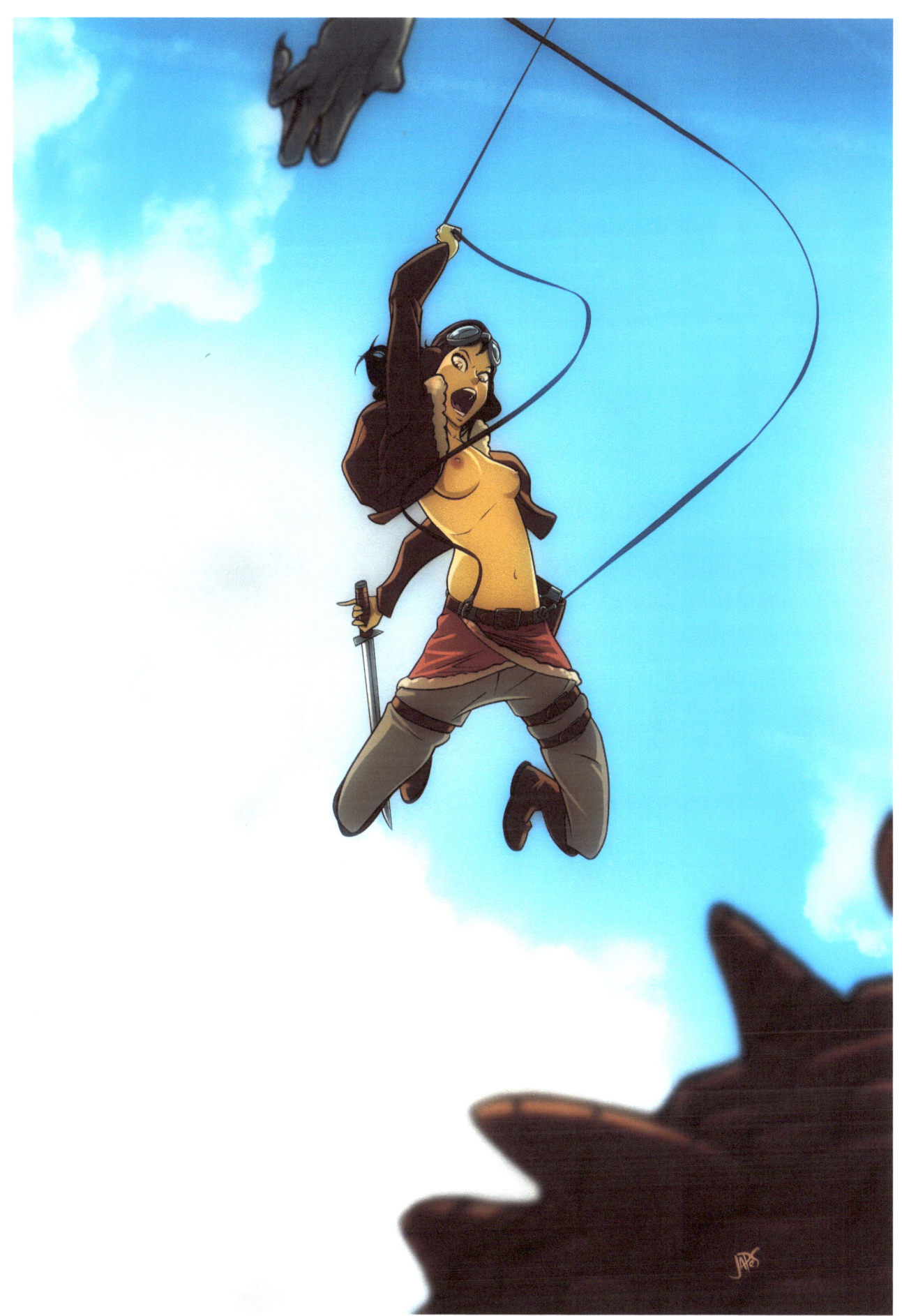

# The Divine Wind Is A Dragon's Breath

From the author of "Scales and Chrome" and "Tentacles and Torpedoes" comes "The Divine Wind Is a Dragon's Breath," a pictorial history of Imperial Japan's kamikaze pilots and dragons during the Second Great War.

"Japan was blessed by a long and fiercely loyal relationship with its vast population of dragons, but not by dragons of great size. As a small island chain in the Pacific, Japan's food chain could not support dragons of a size and strength to rival the behemoths from the West. They, however, compensated for their small size (the largest dragons only able to carry one rider) with a fierceness and devotion to the Empire that shocked and dismayed the Allies.

Few sights were as terrifying for Allied aviators as seeing a lone, small, and swift dragon careen into a bomber dragon in their squadron, followed closely by its rigging and crew falling into the sea, and finally the slow, sad drift away as the immense beast peeled away from formation. For although the Japanese dragon would almost invariably soon drop lifelessly from the sky, unable to survive the power and ferocity of the bigger dragon's counterattack, its suicidal plunge was merely a gambit designed to allow its pilot to clamber onto the Allied dragon's back.

For the Japanese had, early in the war, realized that their populace of dragons, as numerous and proud as they were, were hopelessly outmatched as weapons by their more powerful Western cousins. But, when used as delivery devices for the Kamikaze pilot-- the true weapon-- one tiny dragon with one skilled pilot could neutralize a dragon and crew 10 times its size. Kamikaze pilots were skilled warriors, highly trained in sword and pistol, and unmatched in speed and skill.

It was a testament to that terrible swiftness that Kamikaze pilots were successful as often as they were, for upon alighting upon her target's back, she had to secure her line, cut loose the rigging securing the crew to their dragon with her katana or otherwise kill them with pistol, and then take secure control of the enemy Captain by holding a blade to her throat or pistol to her head, all while dodging small arms fire and keeping from being tossed off by a wildly rolling and bucking dragon. But once she did securely hold the captain hostage, the dragon was hers, so bereft would the Allied dragon be at the loss of his crew and the threat to his Captain's life.

A successful Kamikaze attack thus was a crippling psychological weapon, as it subtracted a powerful weapon from the Allies and added it to the Japanese force. As fiercely loyal as Japanese dragons were to the Emperor, readily laying down their lives in defense of the Empire, so were Allied dragons loyal first and foremost to their Captains (thinking the concept of patriotism rather silly). A Western dragon would not think twice about fighting for the Japanese if it meant keeping his captured Captain safe for the remainder of the war. With this knowledge, even unsuccessful Kamikaze attacks were an effective psychological weapon, as before every mission a Captain would have to look down at her own pistol and think about how she might have to use it. Would she be skilled enough to use it to successfully repel a boarder? And failing that, would she be brave enough to save one last shot for herself, if it meant keeping her dragon out of Japanese hands?"

# Sketches, Alternate Versions, and False Starts

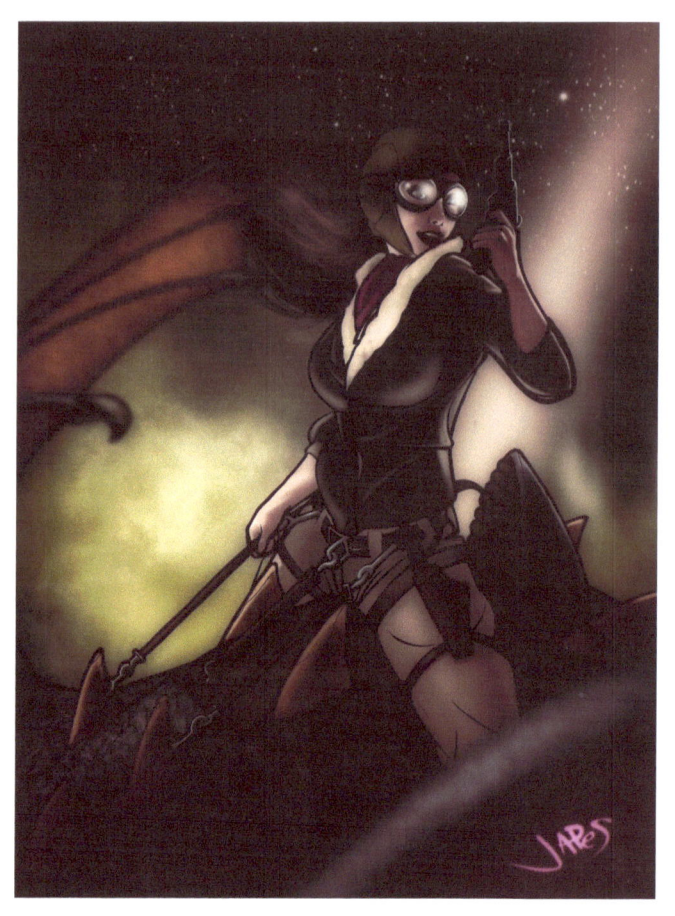

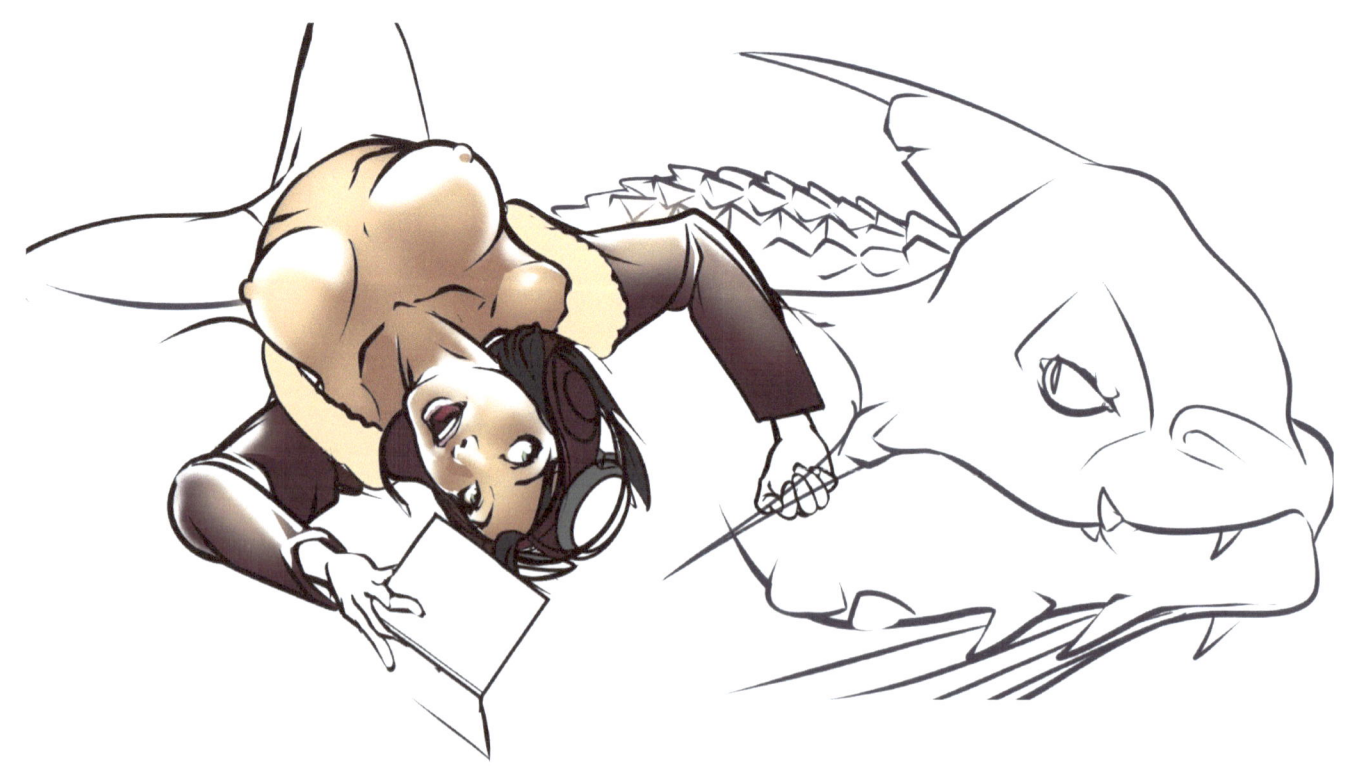

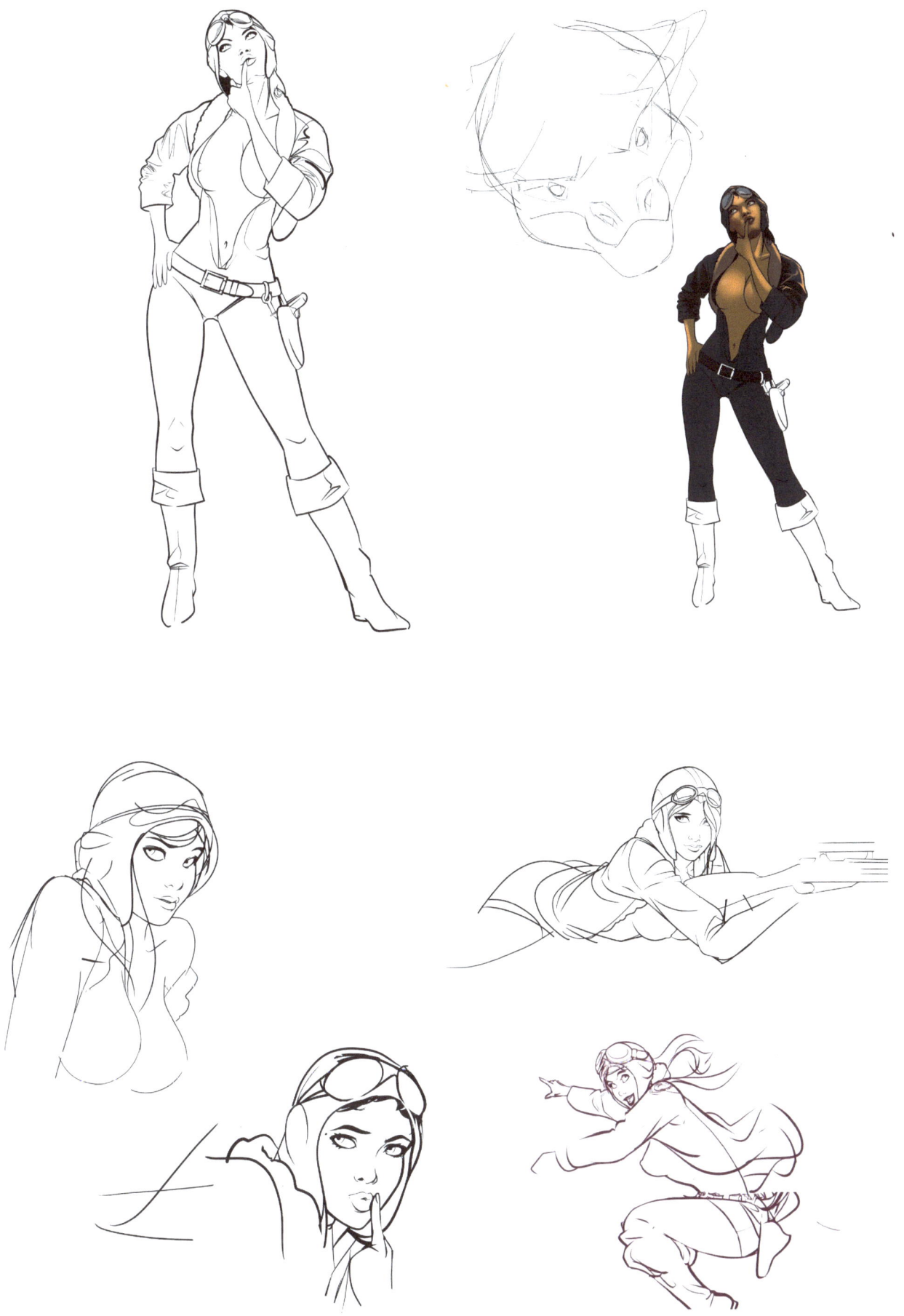

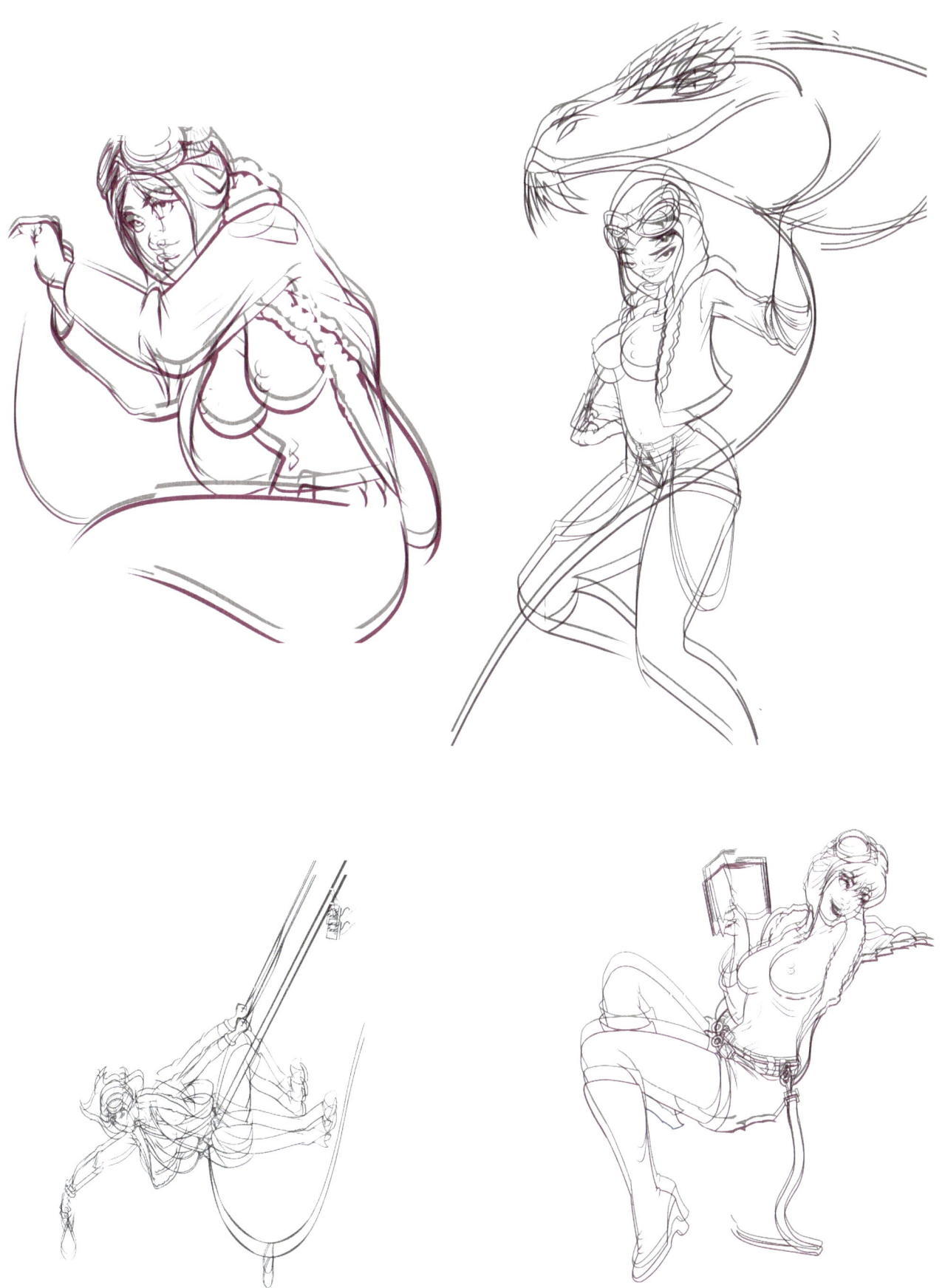

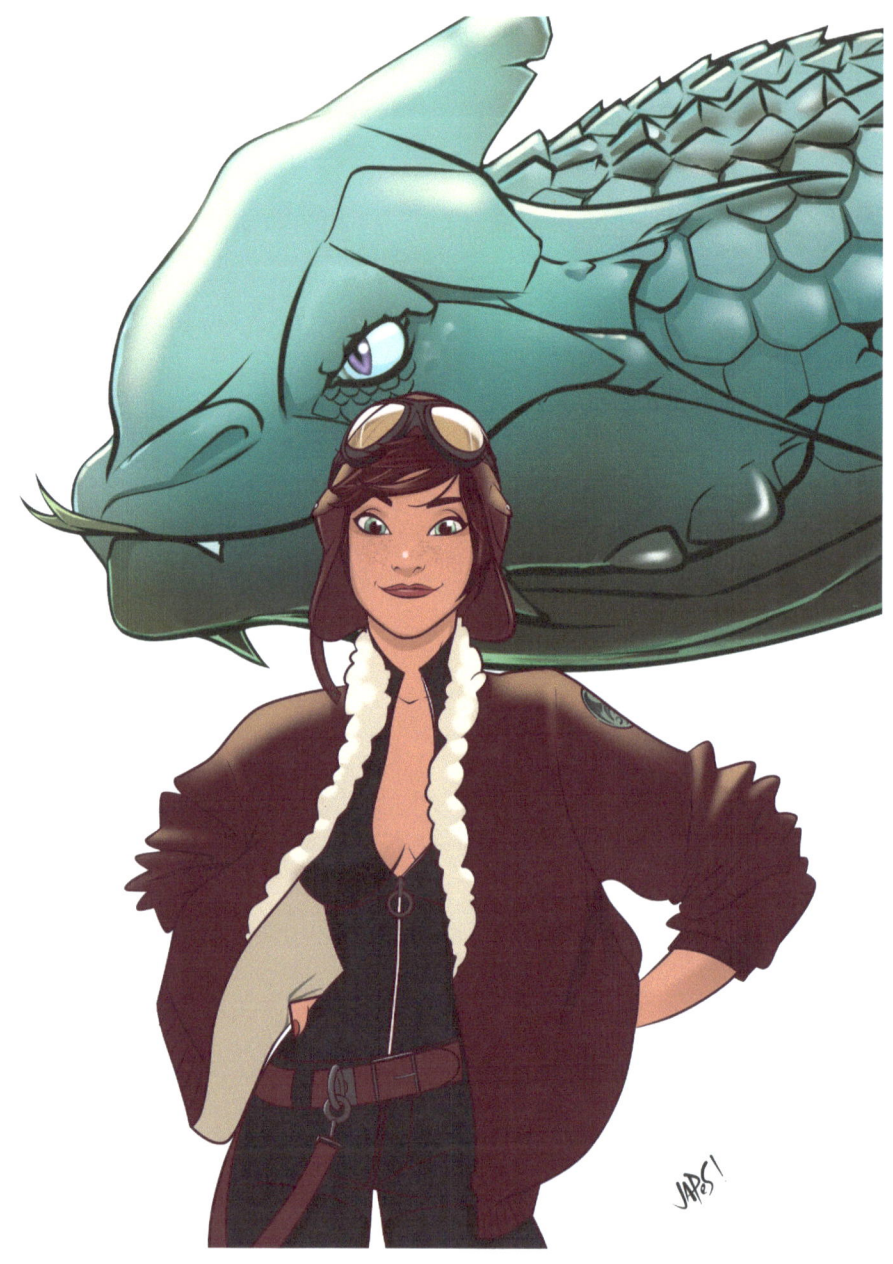

Special Thanks to:
Blakkhat814 for Meredith Brown and Thalassa, and Emma Coleman and nix
Katherine for Lyx Moraine and Tarane
EF for Vanessa and Noir
Judge88 for The Divine Wind
And all my
Patreon supporters who made this book possible!

www.ingramcontent.com/pod-product-compliance
Lightning Source LLC
Chambersburg PA
CBHW051924210526
45473CB00006B/2128